THE LUCENT LIBRARY OF SCIENCE AND TECHNOLOGY

Exploring Mars

by Peggy J. Parks

LUCENT BOOKS

An imprint of Thomson Gale, a part of The Thomson Corporation

Detroit • New York • San Francisco • San Diego • New Haven, Conn. • Waterville, Maine • London • Munich

LIBRARY OF CONGRESS CATALOGING-IN-PUBLICATION DATA

Parks, Peggy J., 1951–
   Exploring Mars / Peggy J. Parks.
      p. cm. — (Lucent library of science & technology)
   Summary: Describes early and current studies of Mars and the future of human exploration of the planet.
   Includes bibliographical references and index.
   ISBN 1-59018-636-2 (hardcover : alk. paper)
   1. Mars (Planet)—Exploration. I. Title. II. Series: Lucent library of science and technology.
   QB641.P37 2004
   629.43'543—dc22

                                                            2004010554

Printed in the United States of America

Table of Contents

Foreword

"The world has changed far more in the past 100 years than in any other century in history. The reason is not political or economic, but technological—technologies that flowed directly from advances in basic science."

— Stephen Hawking, "A Brief History of Relativity," *Time,* 2000

The twentieth-century scientific and technological revolution that British physicist Stephen Hawking describes in the above quote has transformed virtually every aspect of human life at an unprecedented pace. Inventions unimaginable a century ago have not only become commonplace but are now considered necessities of daily life. As science historian James Burke writes, "We live surrounded by objects and systems that we take for granted, but which profoundly affect the way we behave, think, work, play, and in general conduct our lives."

For example, in just one hundred years, transportation systems have dramatically changed. In 1900 the first gasoline-powered motorcar had just been introduced, and only 144 miles of U.S. roads were hard-surfaced. Horse-drawn trolleys still filled the streets of American cities. The airplane had yet to be invented. Today 217 million vehicles speed along 4 million miles of U.S. roads. Humans have flown to the moon and commercial aircraft are capable of transporting passengers across the Atlantic Ocean in less than three hours.

The transformation of communications has been just as dramatic. In 1900 most Americans lived and worked on farms without electricity or mail delivery. Few people had ever heard a radio or spoken on a telephone. A hundred years later, 98 percent of American homes have telephones and televisions and more than 50 percent have personal computers. Some families even have more than one television and computer, and cell phones are now commonplace, even among the young. Data beamed from communication satellites routinely predict global weather conditions, and fiber-optic cable, e-mail, and the Internet have made worldwide telecommunication instantaneous.

Perhaps the most striking measure of scientific and technological change can be seen in medicine and public health. At the beginning of the twentieth century, the average American life span was forty-seven years. By the end of the century the average life span was approaching eighty years, thanks to advances in medicine including the development of vaccines and antibiotics, the discovery of powerful diagnostic tools such as X rays, the lifesaving technology of cardiac and neonatal care, improvements in nutrition, and the control of infectious disease.

Rapid change is likely to continue throughout the twenty-first century as science reveals more about physical and biological processes such as global warming, viral replication, and electrical conductivity, and as people apply that new knowledge to personal decisions and government policy. Already, for example, an international treaty calls for immediate reductions in industrial and automobile emissions in response to studies that show a potentially dangerous rise in global temperatures is caused by human activity. Taking an active role in determining the direction of future changes depends on education; people must understand the possible uses of scientific research and the effects of the technology that surrounds them.

The Lucent Books Library of Science and Technology profiles key innovations and discoveries that have transformed the modern world. Each title strives to make a complex scientific discovery, technology, or phenomenon understandable and relevant to the reader. Because scientific discovery is rarely straightforward, each title explains the dead ends, fortunate accidents, and basic scientific methods by which the research into the subject proceeded. And every book examines the practical applications of an invention, branch of science, or scientific principle in industry, public health, and personal life, as well as potential future uses and effects based on ongoing research. Fully documented quotations, annotated bibliographies that include both print and electronic sources, glossaries, indexes, and technical illustrations are among the supplemental features designed to point researchers to further exploration of the subject.

The Mysterious Red Planet

For thousands of years, people have gazed into the night sky and wondered about the planet Mars. It was an object of particular fascination for ancient astrologers who looked to the heavens for guidance about the past and the future. When they first noticed the fiery red planet, they thought it was a star. But as they continued to study the sky, they discovered that stars appear in fixed patterns (now known as constellations) and traveled across the sky with predictable regularity. Mars, however, and the other "wandering stars" behaved differently. They drifted about the sky from constellation to constellation, as if they were following an invisible path. Because of how these celestial bodies differed from stars, the ancient Greeks named them *planetes*, a word meaning "wanderers."

Although Mars shared certain characteristics with the other planets, sky watchers observed that it was unique in several ways. One difference was its burnished red color, which made it stand out from the rest. Another important feature that made Mars appear different was the way it moved across the sky. Whereas the other planets appeared as a narrow band that traveled in a constant direction, this was not the case with Mars. Instead, after moving in the same direction for many months, Mars began to

The planet Mars, an object of fascination for centuries, appears as a bright light in the night sky.

flare brilliantly and then reverse its course and start traveling backward. Because of its peculiar behavior, along with its fiery red color, Mars was associated with war, violence, danger, and death. As a result, some ancient peoples named the planet after their gods of war. The Greeks called it Ares, and the Romans called it Mars.

Thousands of years have passed since Mars was thought to be a brilliant red star shining in the night sky, but the human fascination with the planet has far from diminished. Since the 1960s, sophisticated technology and modern space missions have provided scientists with a wealth of knowledge and information. Still, many questions remain unanswered. For instance, even though it is doubtful that life exists on Mars today, was there a time when it did? If so, what happened to it? The absence of living things is likely related to the lack of water on the planet, which is another unsolved mystery. Scientists have tangible proof that water once ran freely on Mars, but there appears to be no trace of surface water now. What caused it to disappear?

Why Explore Mars?

As space exploration continues, additional pieces of the Mars puzzle will fall into place. Yet some people question whether it is worthwhile to study Mars at all. Space missions are extremely expensive, costing billions of dollars every year, but scientists are convinced that Mars exploration is crucial and must continue. That is because Mars is quite similar to Earth, and about 4 billion years ago, when the two planets were formed, they may have been almost identical. Geologists believe there was a time when Mars had a warmer and wetter climate, vast quantities of surface water, and an atmosphere that was much like Earth's. Over the course of its history, however, Mars has undergone such drastic changes that it looks as though it is caught in the grip of a global ice age. Today, the planet's surface is dry and lifeless, its atmosphere is unfit for human life, and its average daily temperature is more bone-chilling than even the coldest place on Earth. What caused these drastic changes? And is Earth destined for the same fate? By continuing to explore Mars, scientists

A photograph of Mars reveals a rocky surface that seems devoid of life.

can gain a much greater understanding of the red planet, as well as insight into what the future may hold for Earth.

Mars has always been, and continues to be, a planet shrouded in mystery and intrigue. No one knows with any certainty what future exploration will reveal. But with each new mission, and each piece of knowledge that is gained, Mars becomes even more compelling for those who are determined to uncover its secrets. Astronomer and author William Sheehan shares his thoughts about why ongoing Mars exploration is so important:

> It is a region untenanted and waiting to be claimed and challenged by our ideas. . . . The trailblazers who have led us to Mars have had various sources for their obsessions with the planet. Their obsessions, in turn, have contributed to our ongoing fascination. Some of the Mars-intoxicated ones were heroic figures; others were flawed, though their grand romantic visions often proved to be more inspiring than the truths of narrower minds. All were pioneers, dreaming of a brave new world that was disclosed to their eyes long before they or anyone else could arrive bodily. And so it is that we continue to explore Mars in our hearts and minds, until, one day, we remove Mars from the imagination and make it real.[1]

Chapter 1

Early Observations and Beliefs

In the early 1600s, a wondrous device was introduced in the Netherlands. It featured a tube with glass lenses at opposite ends and was designed for the purpose of making distant objects appear to be closer. Word of the invention, which would later be called the telescope, spread throughout Europe and came to the attention of Galileo Galilei, an Italian scientist. Although Galileo had not seen the device for himself, he became so intrigued with its potential that he designed and built one of his own.

A devout observer of the skies, Galileo intended to use his telescope to study the stars and planets. His model resembled a small pair of binoculars and used an arrangement of glass lenses for magnification. When he looked through it, objects appeared about thirty times larger than their normal size. In 1609 Galileo became the first person to use a telescope for the purposes of astronomy, and he recorded his findings in a book titled *Starry Messenger*.

Differing Scientific Theories

For centuries before Galileo used his telescope, other scientists had been watching the skies and tracking

Seventeenth century Italian scientist Galileo Galilei used a telescope like this one to study the stars and planets.

the movement of Mars and the other planets. One was a Greek astronomer and mathematician named Claudius Ptolemaeus (better known as Ptolemy), who lived in Egypt during the second century A.D. Like most scientists and scholars before him, Ptolemy believed in a geocentric system: that Earth was at the center of the universe, and the sun, planets, moon, and stars all revolved around it. The late astronomer and author Carl Sagan wrote about Earth-centered beliefs in his book *Cosmos:* "This is the most natural idea in the world. The Earth seems steady, solid, immobile, while we can see the heavenly bodies rising and setting each day. Every culture has leaped to the geocentric hypothesis."[2]

In the Middle Ages, Ptolemy's philosophy was widely accepted, and was embraced by the Roman Catholic Church, which believed it to be consistent with biblical principles. Any Catholic whose beliefs opposed the geocentric system was considered guilty of a crime called heresy and could be severely punished. Because of the grave risks involved, even scientists who may have disagreed with Ptolemy dared not speak out. For centuries after his death, Europe paid very little scientific attention to studying the planets.

During the Renaissance, a period of heightened interest in the arts and sciences, some people dared to challenge the Earth-centered theory. One of the most famous was a Polish Catholic cleric named Mikolaj Kopernik, who was more widely known by the Latin name he chose for himself, Nicolaus Copernicus. After thirty years of painstakingly charting the motions of the planets, Copernicus wrote about his findings in a book called *On the Revolutions of the Heavenly Orbs*—and it was clear that his beliefs were radically different from Ptolemy's. According to Copernicus, it was the sun that was at the center of the universe, and all the planets (including Earth) revolved around it. He wrote that no planets or stars orbited Earth, and the only celestial body that did was the moon, which was a satellite rather than a planet. This sun-centered theory became known as the heliocentric system, from the Greek word *helios*, which means "sun."

Copernicus knew his book would be condemned by the Catholic Church, so he chose not to publish it until shortly before his death in 1543. Yet even though his beliefs were a major step toward correcting the erroneous theories of the past, they were far from perfect. For instance, in discussing what he called the "ballet of the planets," Copernicus proposed that each planet orbited in a perfectly circular motion. (Although this was incorrect, it was a common belief at the time.) Another flaw in Copernicus's theories was its inability to explain why the planets moved the way they did or why Mars sometimes did its peculiar backward march across the sky. Because his book left so many unanswered questions, many scientists did not support Copernicus's ideas.

Years of Progress

Several decades after Copernicus's work became public, it attracted the attention of a well-known Danish nobleman and astronomer named Tycho Brahe. Tycho (as he was commonly known) did not agree completely with either Ptolemy or Copernicus, but instead believed there could be a compromise between the geocentric system and the heliocentric system. To observe the skies and chart the movements of the stars and planets, Tycho developed a collection of high-precision instruments. He also founded an observatory on an island located between Denmark and Sweden. The facility, called Uraniborg, came to be known as the finest astronomical observatory in Europe. Among its scientific tools was an instrument called the wall quadrant, which Tycho used to take precise measurements of a celestial object's position in the sky.

Scientists Tycho Brahe (left) and Johannes Kepler (center) had differing opinions about the sun-centered theory put forth by Nicolaus Copernicus (right).

Because of Tycho's keen interest in Mars, he focused on it during many of his observations. He noticed that it appeared to move faster than the other planets, so he could chart its movements more frequently. He was particularly interested in knowing

why Mars reversed directions as it moved across the sky. During his twenty years at Uraniborg, Tycho made thousands of measurements of Mars in its various celestial positions.

Toward the end of the sixteenth century, Tycho closed his observatory and moved to Prague, where he was appointed imperial mathematician, the most prestigious mathematics position in Europe. In 1600 he invited German scientist Johannes Kepler to become his assistant. Unlike Tycho, Kepler firmly believed in Copernicus's theory about a heliocentric universe. In spite of their difference of opinion, however, Kepler had a great deal of respect and admiration for Tycho, so he accepted the offer and joined him in Prague. He then began to work on studying the orbit of Mars.

A Brilliant Scientific Mind

One year after Kepler moved to Prague, Tycho was suddenly stricken with a serious illness. On his deathbed, he pleaded with his assistant to continue with his life's work, saying, "Let me not seem to have lived in vain. . . . Let me not seem to have lived in vain."[3] After Tycho's death, Kepler continued his extensive study of Mars. Over the following years, he proved that Copernicus had been correct: All planets revolve around the sun. One of his findings, though, was particularly astounding—even to him—because it revealed a major flaw in a prevailing scientific belief. Until that point, it was believed that Mars and other planets traveled in circular motions during their orbits. The circle was regarded as the perfect form, and even the most brilliant scientists believed it was impossible for anything less than perfection to guide the movement in the heavens. Kepler himself had shared that belief, but he now knew it was wrong.

During his years of astronomical research, Kepler's calculations had clearly shown that Mars and the other planets did not orbit the sun in a circular pattern at all. Instead, they traveled in the shape of an ellipse, or oval, with the sun off to one side. Kepler found that the shape of a planet's orbit varied based on how close it was to the sun. Those nearest to the sun had a more circular orbit than those farther away. Plus, he noted that a planet's proximity to the sun affected the speed at which it traveled. Because Mars was farther away from the sun than Earth, its orbit time was longer. This discovery was especially profound because it explained why Mars periodically reversed direction in the sky, a phenomenon known as retrograde motion. As Earth traveled along in its orbit, it occasionally passed Mars, which created the illusion that the red planet was moving backward.

In 1609 Kepler announced his findings, which became known as Kepler's laws of motion, and he published a historic book called *Astronomia Nova (New Astronomy)*. Scientist and author Isaac Asimov explains the importance of these revelations: "Kepler's model of the planetary orbits explained the planetary motions so beautifully and simply that there could be no further doubt that all the planets really moved about the Sun. The system of planets therefore came to be called the 'solar system' from the Latin word for 'sun.'"[4]

Galileo's Findings

At the same time that Kepler was making his observations and discoveries, Galileo was using the telescope he had built to get a closer look at the skies. He observed mountains and craters on the moon and spots on the surface of the sun, and he discovered four of Jupiter's moons. Galileo was also able to chart the different phases of the planet Venus, which (like the moon) changed from a full disk to a thin sliver of light. Mars, however, was farther away and not so easily seen. Even though Galileo could see the planet more clearly than was possible with

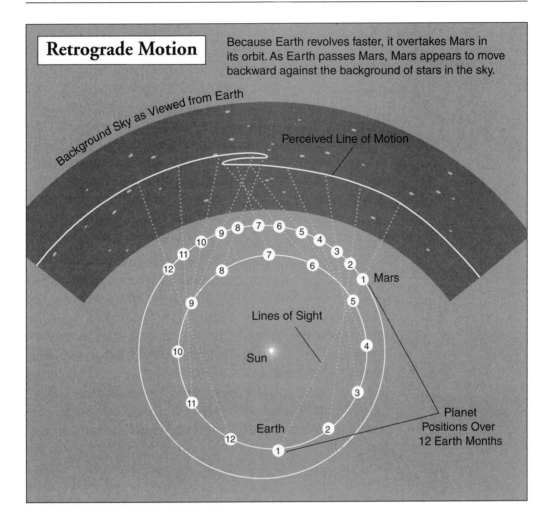

Retrograde Motion

Because Earth revolves faster, it overtakes Mars in its orbit. As Earth passes Mars, Mars appears to move backward against the background of stars in the sky.

Background Sky as Viewed from Earth

Perceived Line of Motion

Mars

Lines of Sight

Sun

Earth

Planet Positions Over 12 Earth Months

the naked eye, his telescope was quite primitive and not very powerful. Therefore, he could not see any surface features, nor was he able to observe the different phases of Mars as he had with Venus. But he was able to distinguish that Mars's diameter seemed to vary at different times, and he described this in a letter to a friend: "I ought not to claim that I can see the phases of Mars; however, unless I am deceiving myself, I believe I have already seen that it is not perfectly round."[5]

Galileo had seen how the appearance of Mars changed based on its proximity to the sun and

Earth. He viewed this as undeniable proof that the planets orbited the sun and that Earth was not the center of the universe. Confident in his newfound knowledge, he began to argue publicly in favor of Copernicus's theory, which was still considered a contradiction of biblical teachings. Even though many years had passed since Copernicus's book had shocked and angered the church, any Catholic who supported his theories was in danger of persecution. As a result of his controversial views, Galileo was accused of being a heretic and put on trial. Much to his relief, he was declared innocent and received only a strong warning not to teach Copernican theory.

Yet even threats from the church could not stop Galileo from continuing to observe the skies with his telescope. In 1632 he published *Dialogue Concerning the Two Chief World Systems*, a book that clearly stated his theory that the universe was not Earth centered. The book infuriated the church, and Galileo was again condemned for beliefs that were considered heresy. At nearly seventy years of age, in order to avoid being tortured and executed, the great scientist denied what he knew was the truth: He publicly stated that he had been wrong to believe that Earth moves around the sun. Galileo's confession saved him from a horrible death, but he lived for the rest of his life under house arrest in his home in Italy.

Decades of Discovery

In the years following Galileo's work with the telescope, scientists developed a heightened interest in studying the skies. One such scientist was Francisco Fontana, an Italian astronomer who produced the first known drawing of Mars in 1636. He continued to study the planet and in 1638 he was able to see its different phases, which he depicted in a second drawing. However, his telescope was only slightly more powerful than Galileo's had been, and he mistook a defect in the lens for variations in the planet's color. As a result, Fontana's drawings did not accurately reflect actual markings on the surface of Mars.

In 1659 a Dutch mathematician and physicist named Christiaan Huygens used his own telescope to observe Mars. Because the model he had built was much more powerful than those used previously, he was able to see a surface feature on the planet that he compared to a large bog. The area, named Syrtis Major, was later confirmed to be one of the darkest

A satellite photograph of Mars shows the white polar ice cap and dark surface feature Syrtis Major seen by early scientists.

volcanic regions on Mars. As Huygens continued to carefully study the dark, triangle-shaped spot, he charted how its position changed over a period of time. From his observations, he was able to determine that the Martian day was nearly identical to Earth's. Also, using mathematical calculations, he estimated that Earth was about 60 percent larger than Mars (later proven to be nearly correct).

Another Italian astronomer who charted the movement of Mars was Giovanni Cassini, who made drawings of what he observed. He determined that the Martian day was slightly longer than Earth's twenty-four-hour day. He also noticed a white spot at the planet's northern tip, which he assumed was a polar cap.

A few years after Cassini had made his discoveries, Huygens found a second polar cap on the southern tip of Mars. In a book called *Cosmotheoros*, he explained his views about the possibility of life on Mars. He believed that even though the planet would be colder than Earth because of its distance from the sun, it was possible for life to adapt and survive there. Huygens's health was failing when he wrote *Cosmotheoros*, and it was not published until 1697, two years after his death. Nevertheless, it was one of the first known publications ever written about extraterrestrial life.

A Clone of the Earth?

Observations of Mars continued during the eighteenth century. In the late 1700s a British astronomer named Sir William Herschel used his own telescopes to intensively study Mars, and he began to see many similarities with Earth. After measuring the orientation of the Martian poles, he discovered that Mars and Earth were tilted at nearly the same angle, which meant that both planets had four different seasons. He could see that the Martian polar caps grew and shrank as the seasons changed, so he concluded that they were made of snow and ice. In addition, Herschel determined that Mars, like Earth, had some sort of atmosphere, and he (mistakenly) identified dark markings on the Martian surface as oceans.

In a paper titled "The Philosophical Transactions," Herschel described the many similarities between his own planet and Mars:

> The analogy between Mars and the earth is, perhaps, by far the greatest in the whole solar system. The [daily] motion is nearly the same; the [slant] of their respective ecliptics, on which the seasons depend, not very different; of all the superior planets the distance of Mars from the sun is by far the nearest alike to that of the earth; nor will the length of the [Martian] year appear very different from that which we enjoy.[6]

Because Mars was so much like Earth, Herschel was convinced that the red planet teemed with populations of living creatures. Some scientists shared his viewpoint, while others thought it was nonsense.

The Story of the Martian Canals

As larger and more powerful telescopes were developed, astronomers continued turning their eyes to the heavens. They paid the most attention during oppositions, which was when Mars and Earth were on the same side of the sun. That was when the two planets were closest together and Mars flared more brightly than ever in the sky. The opposition of 1877 was an especially good time for sky watching because Mars and Earth were about 35 million miles apart—as close as they could possibly be. It was during the summer 1877 opposition that American astronomer Asaph Hall discovered the two moons of Mars. He named them Phobos (fear) and Deimos (terror) after characters in Greek mythology.

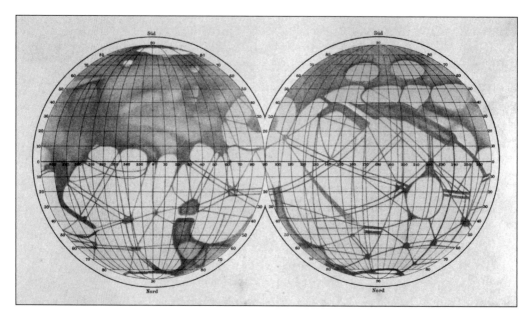

Italian astronomer Giovanni Schiaparelli drew this and other detailed maps of Mars.

Another scientist who was intently watching Mars during the 1877 opposition was an Italian astronomer named Giovanni Schiaparelli. In written reports, he noted the location of more than sixty features on the Martian surface, and he drew detailed maps showing them. However, Schiaparelli reported seeing something else during his studies that resulted in decades of myths about Mars: a network of long, dark lines that crisscrossed the brightest areas of the planet. Other astronomers had noticed lines on the Martian surface in the past, but Schiaparelli was the first to report seeing such an extensive collection of them. He called the lines *canali*, the Italian word for "channels" or "grooves," but the word was mistranslated into English as "canals." This simple error in translation proved to have astounding effects because canals were artificial waterways used for travel, shipping, or irrigation. People throughout the world had become familiar with canals in 1869, when the famous Suez Canal was built to connect the Mediterranean and Red seas. If such waterways existed on Mars, it could mean only one thing—they had been built by some sort of intelligent living beings.

The Martian Frenzy

Word of the Martian "canals" traveled fast and soon became front-page news throughout Europe and America. A headline from an August 12, 1877, editorial in the *New York Times* questioned "Is Mars Inhabited?" and people everywhere wondered what sort of living creatures dwelled on the surface of Earth's neighbor. Noted scientist and writer Sallie Baliunas describes the stir caused by Schiaparelli's announcement:

> Speculation about the canal builders spread wildly. The public wished to believe that advanced civilizations existed on Mars. Their ancient oceans gone, their planet dying, Martians had built elaborate canal systems to survive. Brackish areas like Syrtis Major, whose edges changed over the years, were thought of as seasonal plant growth and retreat irrigated by the canals, instead of the shifting sands they are. . . . Plans were devised for signaling the Martians, despite what was sure to be a formidable impediment in translating between Martian and English.[7]

One man who was particularly struck by Mars fever was an American self-taught astronomer named Percival Lowell. The news of Schiaparelli's discoveries exhilarated Lowell, and he vowed to devote his time, energy, and substantial financial resources to studying Mars. In 1894 he founded a world-class astronomical research observatory in Flagstaff, Arizona, called the Lowell Observatory. Built at an elevation of more than seven thousand feet, where the air was cool and crystal clear, the facility provided Lowell with the best possible view of the night sky, as well as unparalleled opportunities to examine the red planet.

Lowell spent more than ten years studying Mars, and he identified what he believed to be hundreds of canals—many more than Schiaparelli had discovered. In the process of his observations, Lowell determined that the canals were too wide to be the artificial waterways they were thought to be. Instead, he thought they were agricultural regions with irrigation ditches that were fed when seasonal warming caused the polar ice caps to melt. He became convinced that Mars was a place of intelligent beings who were trying desperately to survive on an aging planet that had grown drier and more barren over time.

A 1924 painting reflects the early-twentieth-century belief that intelligent life might exist on Mars.

During the late 1800s and early 1900s, Lowell gave public lectures and wrote articles for such magazines as *Atlantic Monthly* and *Popular Astronomy*. He also published three books: *Mars* (which included his canal maps), *Mars and Its Canals*, and *Mars as the Abode of Life*. Lowell continued to captivate the public with his notions of a living, breathing planet, and newspapers eagerly reported his "discoveries." In 1907 the *Wall Street Journal* published an article that touted "the proof by astronomical observations . . . that conscious, intelligent human life exists upon the planet Mars."[8] A few years later, the *New York Times* ran a story titled "Martians Build Two Immense Canals in Two Years," which described Lowell's alleged discovery of Martian canals that were a thousand miles long and twenty miles wide.

This frenzy over Mars sparked the imagination of fiction writers, some of whom were smitten with the red planet. One such writer was Edgar Rice Burroughs, an author who wrote a series of science fiction books featuring a character named John Carter, who has many adventures on Mars. Another famous author who romanticized the red planet was H.G. Wells, whose book *War of the Worlds* went on to become one of the most famous science fiction books of all time. Wells's book, released in 1898, portrayed Martians as fearsome, brutal, technologically advanced invaders whose mission was to kill thousands of Earth's inhabitants and take control of the planet.

Myths Versus Facts

While the general public was being swept away with enticing stories of Martian life, many scientists had begun to question Lowell's findings. Using telescopes that were larger and more powerful than his, they combed the skies, searching for signs of the Martian canals, and could see no trace of them. They suspected that the extensive collection of lines he had professed seeing were actually caused by two things: normal optical illusions and Lowell's over-active imagination. It was eventually determined that the *canali* seen by Schiaparelli and Lowell were nothing more than natural features and shadows that, when viewed from far away, only seemed to be connected.

In spite of the scientific evidence refuting Lowell's beliefs, he remained convinced that there were intelligent Martians—and canals built by them—until the time of his death in 1916. And even though many of his theories were flawed, to this day he is still considered an important contributor to the heightened awareness of Mars, as noted scientist Robert Zubrin explains:

> We now know that Lowell was absolutely wrong in his investigations of Mars, but he did leave an important legacy behind: he fired the imaginations of people to make them see a world on Mars. True, that world turned out to be wildly inaccurate, but its envisionment led to a massive uplifting of at least a segment of the popular mind. . . . Lowell made Mars habitable in the imagination only, but it is from imagination that reality is created.[9]

Chapter 2

An Earth-Like World

Much has been learned about the planet Mars since astronomers first began studying it with their telescopes. Some scientific findings proved to be factual, while others were found to be myths. Still, the work of early scientists was invaluable. It stimulated people's curiosity and served as the foundation for centuries of Martian exploration and fascinating discoveries.

Similarities with Earth

Throughout history, many people believed that Mars and Earth were twins. Both are terrestrial, or rocky, planets rather than gaseous. Both have atmospheres and surface features such as towering mountains, deep canyons, and valleys, as well as ice caps at both the northern and southern poles. Also, as Sir William Herschel discovered in the 1700s, both planets are tilted at similar angles: Earth at 23.45 degrees, and Mars at 25.19 degrees. Because of this tilt, certain areas of Mars and Earth are oriented toward the sun at different times of the year; as a result, both planets have four separate seasons.

Another similarity between Mars and Earth is the length of their days. An Earth day lasts for twenty-four hours, because that is how long it takes for

Earth to make one complete spin on its axis while it travels around the sun. A Martian day is nearly identical, lasting for twenty-four hours, thirty-nine minutes, and thirty-five seconds. So, someone standing on Mars would see the sun rising in the morning, climbing in the sky during the day, and setting in the evening, just as it appears to do on Earth.

Stark Differences

Yet even though Mars is more like Earth than any other planet in the solar system, the two planets are different in many ways. One dissimilarity is the length of their years. An Earth year lasts for 365 days, which is how long it takes the planet to travel around the sun. Mars is about one and a half times

Earth		Mars
7,928 miles	DIAMETER	4217 miles
23.45°	PLANETARY TILT	25.19°
24 hours	ONE ROTATION AROUND AXIS (ONE DAY)	24 hours 39 minutes 35 seconds
365 days	ONE ORBIT AROUND THE SUN (ONE YEAR)	687 days

farther from the sun, so its orbit takes longer—687 days—which means the Martian year is nearly twice as long as Earth's. One result of the longer year is that seasons on Mars last nearly twice as long as they do on Earth. Also, Earth's faster orbit means that it is constantly gaining on Mars, and passes the planet about every twenty-six months. These close encounters, known as oppositions, occur when Earth and Mars are closest together. But because of their elliptical orbits, the distance between them is never exactly the same. Typically, they are from 60 million miles to more than 300 million miles apart, but during oppositions they are much closer. For example, on August 27, 2003, Mars was 34,654,500 miles from Earth—closer than it has been in thousands of years.

As for size and gravitational force, Mars and Earth are nothing alike. With a diameter of 4,217 miles, Mars is only about half the size of Earth. The smaller size affects the planet's gravity, which is only about 38 percent as strong as Earth's. So, someone who weighs two hundred pounds on Earth would weigh a mere seventy-six pounds on Mars. Despite the size differences between the two planets, the surface area of Mars is roughly the same size as the land area of Earth. That is because approximately 70 percent of Earth is covered by oceans, and these vast bodies of water do not exist on Mars.

A Rugged, Rocky Planet

Although the terrain on Mars is more like Earth's than any other planet's, it is extremely rugged and desertlike. Much of the Martian surface is covered with thick, powdery soil that has the consistency of flour, and the ground is strewn with jagged rocks and boulders of all shapes and sizes. After viewing close-up photographs of Mars, some people have described the planet as lifeless and desolate, but the late Carl Sagan viewed it in a very different way: "The landscape is stark and red and lovely: boulders thrown out in the creation of a crater somewhere over the horizon, small sand dunes, rocks that have been repeatedly covered and uncovered by drifting dust, plumes of fine-grained material blown about by the winds."[10] The red landscape Sagan referenced is one of Mars's most distinctive features. Because of a high iron oxide (rust) content in the soil, its color ranges from brownish-yellow to deep, dark red. This gives the whole planet a reddish tinge, hence the nickname "red planet."

There are striking differences between the southern and northern regions of Mars. The southern two-thirds of the planet is mostly highlands, and is dominated by huge impact craters that were formed when asteroids and comets struck the planet. Hellas Planitia, the largest and deepest of all the Martian craters, is nearly four miles deep and over twelve hundred miles wide. Heavily cratered land is typically billions of years old, so the southern area is believed to be the most ancient terrain on Mars. Since the northern third of the planet is only lightly cratered, it is thought to be much younger. The area is covered with diverse geological features such as volcanoes, channels, plains, and valleys. Geologists believe the volcanoes are currently dormant, although they do not know what caused the eruptions to stop. There is evidence that some became inactive several billion years ago, while others erupted much more recently. Astronomer William K. Hartmann explains the significance of this: "Some individual flow units could be as young as 10 million years or less. In geological terms, that's so recent that volcanic activity might start up again at any time somewhere on the red planet."[11]

The northern hemisphere of Mars is home to the Tharsis Bulge, an expansive volcanic region that rises six miles above the Martian surface and covers an area as large as North America. There are many volcanoes in the Tharsis area, including some so massive that they dwarf any volcanoes found on Earth. Scientists cannot say for sure why Martian volcanoes grow to be so large, but they believe it is because Mars's surface does not consist of separate crustal plates as Earth's does. This phenomenon, known as plate tectonics, means that Earth is constantly on the move, with new crust forming and old crust being swallowed up. Such ongoing movement causes constant changes in Earth's crust and inhibits how large volcanoes can grow. Although plate tectonics may have played a role in shaping Mars very early in the planet's history, scientists can tell that the Martian crust has remained exactly the same for billions of years. California Institute of Technology professor David Stevenson explains: "The lack of plate tectonics on Mars limited the planet's ability to recycle material. Four billion year old rocks are fairly common there."[12] Because Mars is such a stationary planet, its volcanoes have been undisturbed as they grew to towering heights.

The most enormous volcano on Mars, Olympus Mons, is located in the Tharsis region. Olympus Mons is a shield volcano, a type of volcano that was

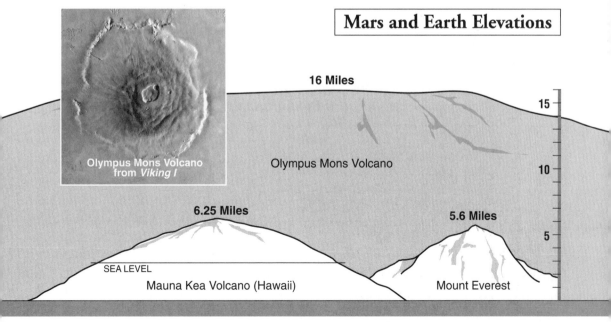

Mars and Earth Elevations

16 Miles

15

Olympus Mons Volcano from *Viking I*

Olympus Mons Volcano

10

6.25 Miles

5.6 Miles

5

SEA LEVEL

Mauna Kea Volcano (Hawaii)

Mount Everest

formed by smoothly flowing lava rather than by violent eruptions. At 16 miles high and 370 miles across, it is three times higher than Mount Everest, which is the tallest mountain on Earth. Yet despite its immense height, the volcano has a gentle slope and is nearly as flat as a pancake on top.

Another gigantic Tharsis volcano is Alba Patera, which is believed to be the oldest and broadest volcano on Mars. Alba Patera is more than nine hundred miles across and covers a much wider area than Olympus Mons, although it stands only about one-fourth as high. A relatively small Tharsis volcano is Ceraunius Tholus. Even though it is much smaller than most of its neighbors, it is still about the same size as the island of Hawaii.

In addition to volcanoes, another amazing geological feature in the Tharsis area of Mars is a massive canyon system known as Valles Marineris. This geological wonder was formed billions of years ago when pressure within the planet's interior caused the crust to swell and split open, creating immense gashes in the surface. The canyon system is three thousand miles long, five miles deep, and in some places more than four hundred miles wide. If Valles Marineris were on Earth, it would stretch across the entire United States and make the Grand Canyon look like nothing more than a tiny crevice in the ground.

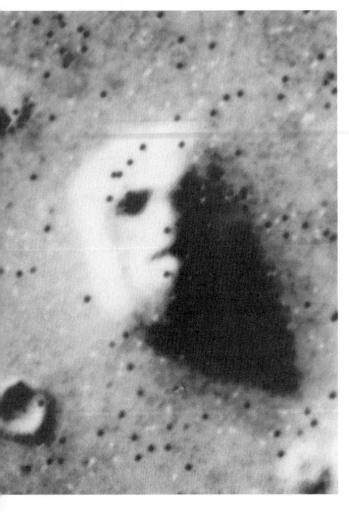

A satellite photo shows the "face" on Mars, one of several of the planet's volcanic surface features.

From Crescents to Ripples

Another geologically unique feature on Mars is its sand dunes, which are found in many different areas of the planet. The most common types are crescent-shaped barchan dunes and steep ridges of sand known as transverse dunes. Photographs have also shown Martian dunes in unusual shapes that people have likened to sharks' teeth, fish scales, chocolate candy kisses, or horseshoe crabs. A particularly interesting photo taken by a spacecraft during the summer of 2003 showed what looked like entire fields of fortune cookies made of sand. These odd shapes are created by the direction and strength of the Martian winds, which also influence the size of the dunes. Some are small sand hills, while others stretch more than three hundred feet into the Martian sky. Their color can vary, but most dunes on Mars are dark because of the color of the minerals that make up Martian sand.

The most expansive area of dunes is found in the northern hemisphere of Mars. Sometimes referred to as a "sea of sand," the massive dune field surrounds the north polar cap and covers nearly 250,000 square miles. Photos taken by National Aeronautics and Space Administration (NASA) spacecraft have confirmed that many northern Martian dunes are active, which means they grow, shrink, and move based on the force and direction of the wind. However, a rare grouping of dunes discovered in an area known as the Herschel Basin have rough, deeply grooved surfaces. Unlike dunes that are composed of loose sand, these look as though they are cemented together.

Other sand formations on Mars are categorized as sand ripples rather than dunes. These ripples are usually found in low-lying areas and inside craters, and can reach heights of about twenty feet, which is in stark contrast to those on Earth, where sand ripples are usually no more than a few feet high.

Scientists believe that the main reason Martian sand ripples grow so tall is that the gravity on Mars is so weak that they are not as likely to collapse from gravitational pull.

Mars from the Inside Out

After years of intensive study, scientists have gained a wealth of knowledge about Mars. There are still many unknowns, though, and one of them is the exact composition of the planet's interior structure. Scientists cannot analyze the Martian interior in the same way they analyze Earth's: by reviewing seismological data, which is the measurement of earthquake activity. Because that sort of information is not yet available about Mars, researchers must analyze statistics about the planet's size, mass, and gravity; compare this data with information that is known about Earth; and form opinions based on what they have learned. So far, studying the Martian interior has not been an exact science, and it has resulted in conclusions that are based on a combination of facts and scientific inferences.

Scientists believe that Mars, like Earth, has an interior that consists of three layers: an inner shell (the core), a middle shell (the mantle), and an outermost layer (the crust). Although there is little information available about the composition of the Martian crust, scientists do have some theories about its size. They believe it varies from about nine miles thick to eighty miles thick in the area of the Tharsis Bulge. Based on this information, even at its thinnest point Mars's crust is thicker than Earth's crust, which ranges from four to twenty-five miles thick. The Martian crust is also believed to be more rigid than Earth's.

The presence of volcanoes and the evidence of solidified lava formations in many areas of Mars are strong indications that there is a mantle beneath the planet's crust. As extreme pressure built up in the mantle, the molten rock forced its way up through

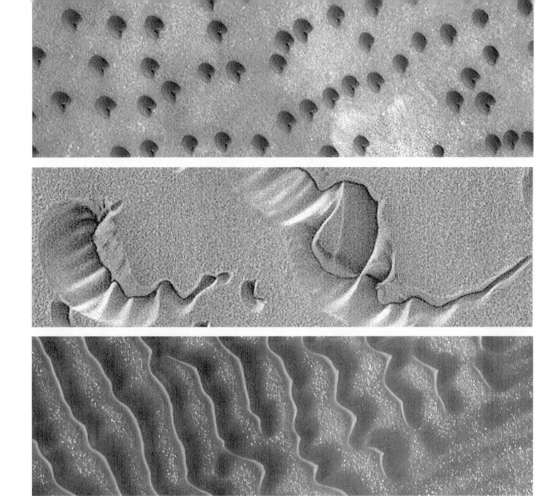

the crust, forming such surface features as the Tharsis Bulge, volcanoes, and deep valleys like Valles Marineris. No one knows the exact composition of Mars's mantle, but geologists believe it is similar to Earth's: a dense, molten-hot layer of semisolid rock that is about the consistency of melted plastic.

Of all the elements that make up the interior of Mars, scientists are most certain about the planet's core. That is because spacecraft have taken measurements of Mars's moment of inertia, a gauge of how a planet's rotation on its axis is influenced by the distribution of mass inside it. Based on these findings, scientists have concluded that there is something dense in the center and something less dense in the outer layers, and that the Martian core has a radius of between 930 and 1,300 miles. They cannot say for sure whether the core is liquid or solid, but unlike

Oddly shaped sand dunes (top and bottom) and craters (middle) are common on the Martian surface.

Mars's Interior Structure

MANTLE
Dense, molten rock.

CORE
Probably solid
or partly solid.

CRUST
Varies from nine to eighty miles thick.

Earth, which has a magnetic field created by the constant motion of its liquid outer core, Mars has little or no magnetic field. That is a likely sign that its core is solid or partly solid.

Harsh Atmosphere and Climate

Much more is known about the atmosphere of Mars than about the planet's interior. Spacecraft have been able to take precise measurements, which have shown that the atmospheres of Mars and Earth are radically different. In fact, if any humans set foot on the red planet, they would not be able to breathe. One reason is that the Martian atmosphere is composed almost entirely of carbon dioxide (CO_2), a colorless, odorless gas that, when inhaled in large, concentrated amounts, is deadly to humans. On Mars, the atmospheric CO_2 level is more than 95 percent, whereas on Earth it is less than 1 percent. The remaining gases in the Martian atmosphere include small percentages of nitrogen and argon and mere traces of oxygen and water vapor. In comparison, the abundant gases in Earth's atmosphere are nitrogen (78 percent) and oxygen (21 percent).

The atmosphere on Mars is also extremely thin—thinner than the atmosphere nineteen miles above Earth—so it cannot filter out the ultraviolet radiation from the sun that is deadly to living matter. Research scientist Paul Withers describes another effect of the thin Martian atmosphere: "It weighs about one percent of what Earth's nitrogen-oxygen atmosphere weighs. So atmospheric pressure on Mars is much lower than on Earth. If you blew up a balloon on Earth and released it on Mars, it would explode immediately because there would be hardly any atmosphere pushing back against it."[13]

Because of the great distance from Mars to the sun, the planet's climate is extremely cold, and there are vast differences between surface temperatures and atmospheric temperatures. For instance, daytime temperatures near the Martian equator can reach 60 or 70 degrees Fahrenheit at the surface level, but just a few feet higher the temperature is only about 15 degrees. Average temperatures at the poles can dip to less than –200 degrees. The planet's frigid climate is also affected by the shape of its orbit around the sun, which is much more elliptical than Earth's. This causes a wide variation in the amount of sunlight that reaches the surface. For instance, when Mars is closest to the sun (a period known as perihelion), the planet receives 40 percent more sunlight than during

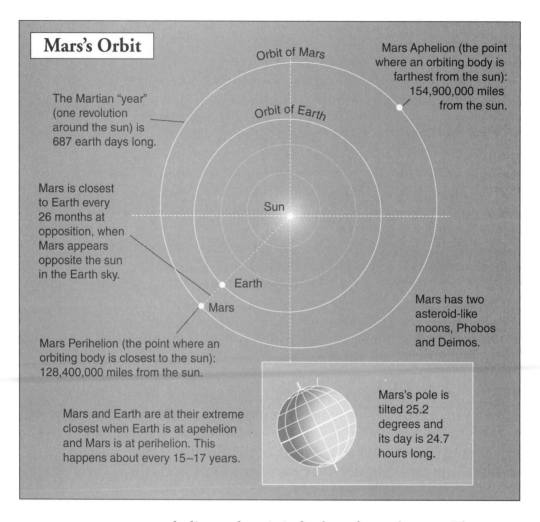

Mars's Orbit

Orbit of Mars

Orbit of Earth

Sun

Earth

Mars

The Martian "year" (one revolution around the sun) is 687 earth days long.

Mars Aphelion (the point where an orbiting body is farthest from the sun): 154,900,000 miles from the sun.

Mars is closest to Earth every 26 months at opposition, when Mars appears opposite the sun in the Earth sky.

Mars Perihelion (the point where an orbiting body is closest to the sun): 128,400,000 miles from the sun.

Mars has two asteroid-like moons, Phobos and Deimos.

Mars and Earth are at their extreme closest when Earth is at apehelion and Mars is at perihelion. This happens about every 15–17 years.

Mars's pole is tilted 25.2 degrees and its day is 24.7 hours long.

aphelion, when it is farthest from the sun. Thus, seasons on Mars are more extreme than seasons on Earth.

The Martian climate is also influenced by the composition of its atmosphere: Because the atmosphere is so thin, it cannot hold heat from the sun. This, combined with the fact that Mars has no oceans to store and distribute solar heat, causes temperatures to fluctuate wildly. They rise quickly when the Martian surface heats up and then plummet when the sun has gone down and its heat escapes back into space.

Volatile Weather

The extreme temperature fluctuations on Mars influence the circulation of its atmosphere, which can result in chaotic and sudden weather changes. The Space Telescope Science Institute describes how radical these weather changes can be:

> If you think the weather on Earth is unpredictable, try living on Mars. One week, the sky is pink and cloudless, filled with windblown dust raised from the rusty Martian surface. By Martian standards, it's warm, about minus 40 degrees Fahrenheit. Then, in a matter of days, the dust is swept from the atmosphere, temperatures plummet 40 degrees, and brilliant water ice clouds appear against a dark blue sky. Dramatic weather changes like these may not seem very different from a batch of severe thunderstorms passing through your home town, but for Mars these changes can sweep over the entire planet every week.[14]

The "windblown dust" refers to Martian dust storms, which are far more severe than any storms on Earth. Strong winds, reaching speeds of up to a hundred miles per hour, churn up dust and sweep it high into the atmosphere, where it grows into massive dust clouds that can cover the skies with a thick reddish haze. As the dust absorbs energy from the sun, it heats the atmosphere, causing temperatures to rise as much as fifty degrees.

The biggest Martian dust storm that scientists have ever observed occurred in June 2001, and it completely blanketed the planet for three months. According to NASA scientist Phil Christensen, the storm began as a small dust cloud inside an impact crater in the southern hemisphere of Mars. It then "exploded" and started growing fast. At its peak, the dust storm made it impossible for scientists to see the Martian surface, but they still felt fortunate to have observed it. Christensen explains why: "Atmospheric scientists have been waiting for a beautiful storm like this. The data we're collecting are marvelous, and I suspect there will be a rush of papers in the months ahead answering some of the questions we have about these events."[15]

Clouds are another common weather-related phenomenon on Mars. Even though the Martian atmosphere contains barely any trace of water vapor, there is enough to cause ice crystals to form when the temperature is at its coldest. When these ice crystals combine with dust particles suspended in the atmosphere, clouds form. Depending on where they form and the color of the soil in the area, clouds may be white, yellow, brown, or pinkish-red, and they resemble waves, plumes, streaks, or puffs of cotton. When clouds form in low areas such as valleys, canyons, and craters, they hover close to the ground in the form of fog or haze. Clouds typically appear in the Martian sky in the early morning and then disappear as the sun warms the planet during the day.

A Waterless World

Clouds hovering above the Martian landscape are one of the rare sources of water on the red planet. The only other place where (frozen) water is known to exist is in the northern and southern polar caps. For years, scientists believed the polar caps were made of frozen carbon dioxide (commonly known as dry ice) rather than water ice. However, findings collected by sophisticated laser instruments proved that theory to be incorrect. Scientists now know that both polar caps are made of thick mounds of water ice, which are covered with thinner blankets of fine dry-ice crystals. The CO_2 covering is considered a seasonal cap because it continuously grows and shrinks based on the season. For instance, during the southern hemisphere's summer (which begins in late September), temperatures become warmer, which

causes the dry ice on the southern polar cap to
"melt" or vaporize, sending CO_2 back into the atmosphere. During the same period, it is winter on
the opposite side of Mars. The resulting cold temperatures cause atmospheric CO_2 to freeze, which in-
creases the size of the seasonal cap and causes the
northern polar cap to expand.

Because the Martian atmospheric pressure is so low
and the temperatures are so extreme, it is not possible for liquid water to exist on the planet today. If
any water managed to make its way to the surface, it
would immediately boil away, or vaporize. However,
scientists believe that was not always the case.
Photographs of Mars have clearly shown deep gullies,
channels, long twisting valleys, and other surface indentations that are likely the remains of ancient
riverbeds, ponds, lakes, or even vast oceans. After analyzing evidence gathered by spacecraft, scientists are
now certain that water was once abundant on Mars.
Many think water may still exist, but probably in the
form of springs or permafrost (permanently frozen
ground) hidden beneath the planet's surface.

Even though Mars is barren and desertlike today,
the knowledge that water once ran freely across the
planet opens up an intriguing possibility: that some
form of life once existed there. Robert Zubrin explains why he is one of the scientists who subscribes
to that theory:

> All creatures great and small surviving in ex-
> treme environments have one thing in com-
> mon: their environment includes a source of wa-
> ter, however meager. The fact that Mars shows a
> remarkable amount of evidence of both surface
> and subsurface water in its distant past argues for
> the possibility of life in the past or perhaps even
> now in an unexpected "Garden of Eden."[16]

Chapter 3

The Space Race

Long before the existence of spacecraft, people were dreaming about the day when exploring Mars would be possible. Even the most sophisticated, high-powered telescopes could not reveal close enough views of the red planet to thoroughly understand it. For that, it would take powerful rockets that could blast off from Earth, spiral millions of miles through space, and get close enough to Mars to actually study it.

Rocket Science

One person who dreamed of Mars exploration from a young age was Robert Goddard. After reading H.G. Wells's novel *War of the Worlds*, Goddard had become enchanted with the idea of space flight. At the age of sixteen he recorded his thoughts in a diary: "It was one of the quiet, colorful afternoons of sheer beauty which we have in October in New England, and as I looked toward the fields at the east, I imagined how wonderful it would be to make some device which had even the *possibility* of ascending to Mars, and how it would look on a small scale, if sent up from the meadow at my feet."[17] Determined to build such a device, Goddard began to design rockets. He launched his first creation in 1926 from his aunt's farm. Even though the small rocket rose just forty-one feet and stayed in the air for only two and a half seconds, it was the first rocket ever propelled by liquid fuel.

Throughout the years, Goddard continued to develop more rocket designs, one of which was the world's first multistage rocket. His concept was based on the principle that a spacecraft could gain the greatest speed and altitude if it were propelled into space by a large rocket and one or more small rockets. After providing the necessary power, the large rocket would jettison, or drop off. Relieved of the extra weight, the spacecraft could then accelerate and continue on its way, jettisoning additional rockets if necessary during the flight. The multistage rocket went on to become one of the most important inventions of space exploration.

Robert Goddard (pictured) began designing primitive rockets like this one during the 1920s.

While Goddard was developing rockets on the East Coast, a group of young men on the opposite side of the country were doing their own experiments. The group established an aeronautics laboratory at the California Institute of Technology in Pasadena, which later became known as the Jet Propulsion Laboratory (JPL). They built both solid-fuel and liquid-fuel rockets, initially for U.S. military use during World War II. In 1958, when JPL became affiliated with the newly created NASA, it assumed the mission of specializing in exploring the solar system beyond Earth.

The Race Begins

Goddard and the JPL group were designing rockets at a time when the world was becoming more focused on space exploration. By international agreement, July 1957 to December 1958 was declared as the International Geophysical Year (IGY), a time devoted to worldwide study of Earth, including its oceans, atmosphere, and solar system. Several years before, the United States had announced its plans to rocket-launch a tiny artificial satellite during IGY. The satellite would be fitted with equipment that could map Earth's surface from space.

The USSR also announced a plan to launch a satellite, but the United States did not take the announcement seriously. It was not aware of the Soviets' progress in developing long-distance rockets such as the *Semiorka*, which was powered by twenty engines. So on October 4, 1957, when *Semiorka* launched a satellite called *Sputnik* into orbit, the world—especially the United States—was caught off guard. *Sputnik* was equipped with instruments such as a thermometer and radio transmitters, and once it reached its orbit, it began circling Earth and transmitting atmospheric information back to Moscow. Before *Sputnik* had completed its journey through space, the USSR launched a second satellite, *Sputnik 2*, that was six times larger than the first. This satellite also contained a passenger, a dog named Laika. Unfortunately, Laika died just four days after launch when the cabin overheated, and *Sputnik 2*'s batteries failed after only six days in space. But even in the face of that failure the Soviets had proven something to the world: The race to explore the skies had begun, and they were clearly in the lead.

The Soviet victory was seen as America's failure. It was glaring proof that the USSR had accomplished what America was not yet able to do. Also, the satellite mission was perceived as a threat to the United States because of hostilities between the two superpowers, as science journalist Paul Raeburn explains: "It was a dazzling engineering achievement, and it was a powerful Cold War victory, raising fears in the United States that the Soviets might have the capability to strike the United States with a nuclear missile launched from Europe."[18]

America in Space

In response to the Soviet Union's progress, the United States accelerated efforts to launch its own satellite. On December 6, 1957, the *Vanguard*, a rocket built by a U.S. Navy team, blasted off from Florida's Cape Canaveral. However, it failed to develop enough power to lift off the launching pad and toppled over on its side, exploding into flames. It was a crushing blow for America, but JPL engineers quickly began working on a second spacecraft called *Orbiter*. This was a different kind of project for the group because instead of building a rocket, as had been JPL's previous focus, this would be a satellite designed to sit on top of a separate missile. Once the satellite was launched, it would separate from its launch vehicle and float in space on its own.

On January 31, 1958, a rocket supplied by the U.S. Army blasted off into space, carrying its payload: America's first artificial satellite, renamed *Explorer 1*.

The bullet-shaped satellite, which weighed just thirty pounds, encircled Earth every 114.8 minutes, for a total of twelve and a half orbits per day. During its time in space, the satellite transmitted information about atmospheric temperatures and radiation, as well as the presence of tiny meteorites called micrometeorites (often called shooting stars). The last transmission was received from *Explorer* on May 23, 1958, nearly four months after its launch.

America had entered the space race, but there was much work to be done before probes (exploratory spacecraft) could be sent to Mars. One of NASA's biggest challenges was charting

America launched its first artificial satellite, Explorer 1, *in January 1958.*

the best path, or trajectory, for a spacecraft to follow on its journey. Timing was critical because in order to reduce the need for fuel, as well as keeping the trip as short as possible, launches needed to coincide with oppositions. This limited time span was known as the launch window; it started about fifty days before each opposition and lasted no more than four weeks. If the opportunity were missed, the next mission would have to wait two more years. NASA's Ron Koczor explains how trajectories work and why they are so important:

Rockets are barely powerful enough to cover the vast distances in interplanetary space, so trajectories are always chosen to make maximum use of the relative motions and positions of Earth and the target planet. For instance, when Mars and Earth are in opposition—meaning lined up and on the same side of the sun—they are closest to each other, and closer is better for fuel-guzzling rockets. Launches are planned so spacecraft can arrive sometime around opposition. Another thing to remember is that for most of its journey to Mars, the spacecraft is coasting. As it leaves Earth, it accelerates to escape velocity [how fast an object must travel to escape from the pull of Earth's gravity] and then the engines are cut off until the ship approaches Mars. When the spacecraft arrives, its engines are used to slow it down until Mars's gravity can capture it. There may be minor course corrections during flight, but these are usually short bursts of power to maintain the correct path.[19]

Another critical issue NASA had to consider when planning a Mars mission was spacecraft design. The rocket needed to be large enough to accommodate a collection of heavy equipment but still light enough to lift off the launching pad and propel the spacecraft during its journey. Also, it had to be shielded from the extreme friction of Earth's and Mars's atmospheres, which creates temperatures as hot as the surface of the sun. As NASA scientists prepared for Mars exploration, they decided to send two spacecraft on all future missions because the chances were greater that at least one would arrive at its destination intact.

Failed Martian Pursuits

While the Americans were addressing the challenges of the first U.S. Mars mission, the Soviets were aggressively pursuing their own Mars exploration

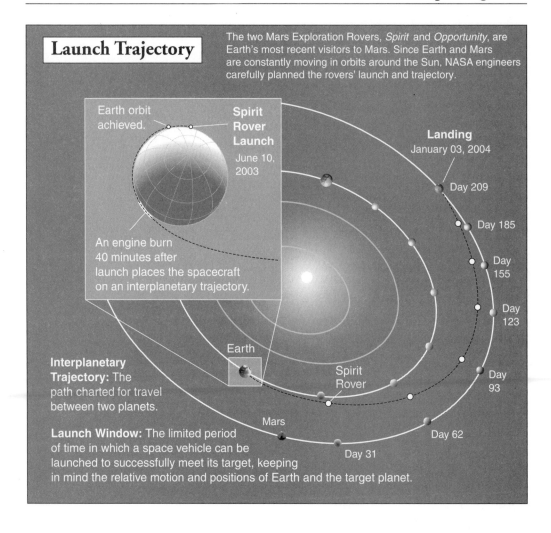

Launch Trajectory

The two Mars Exploration Rovers, *Spirit* and *Opportunity*, are Earth's most recent visitors to Mars. Since Earth and Mars are constantly moving in orbits around the Sun, NASA engineers carefully planned the rovers' launch and trajectory.

Earth orbit achieved.

Spirit Rover Launch
June 10, 2003

An engine burn 40 minutes after launch places the spacecraft on an interplanetary trajectory.

Landing
January 03, 2004

Day 209

Day 185

Day 155

Day 123

Earth

Spirit Rover

Day 93

Interplanetary Trajectory: The path charted for travel between two planets.

Day 62

Mars

Day 31

Launch Window: The limited period of time in which a space vehicle can be launched to successfully meet its target, keeping in mind the relative motion and positions of Earth and the target planet.

goals—and once again they were in the lead. During October 1960, the USSR attempted two missions known as flybys, so named because a spacecraft would fly past Mars rather than attempting to circle the planet or land on it. In both cases, the spacecraft failed to achieve their orbits and were lost. Two years later the Soviets attempted three more missions that were no more successful than their predecessors. The first spacecraft broke apart soon after reaching its orbit, and the impact sent debris whirling through the atmosphere. All contact was lost with the second spacecraft when it was about 66 million miles from

Earth, and the third was destroyed before it exited Earth's atmosphere.

The Soviets refused to give up on their goal of Mars exploration, but their efforts were rewarded with one dismal failure after another. A probe launched in 1964 was nearing Mars when transmissions suddenly stopped and it was presumed lost. Two more space-craft were launched in 1969; the first caught fire and exploded during its ascent into space, and the second failed almost immediately after liftoff.

The First Mars Rovers

After years of failed attempts, the Soviet Union's luck seemed to change when two spacecraft reached Mars in 1971. The first, called *Mars 2*, was launched on May 19, while *Mars 3* followed a few days later. These probes were unlike any that had been launched be-fore, because each was composed of two parts: an or-biter that would orbit Mars and a lander that would be released by the orbiter onto the planet's surface. Once each lander was on the ground, panels would open up to reveal a small roving vehicle designed to scoot along the planet's surface by using skis attached to its sides. Both "rovers" were fitted with scientific instruments for measuring the chemical properties of the soil and the composition of the atmosphere. They were also equipped with mechanical scoops to search for organic signs of life and cameras to photo-graph the Martian surface.

The Soviet mission started out well, but it did not go according to plan. *Mars 2* crashed while attempt-ing to land, and although *Mars 3* managed to land successfully, its transmissions back to Moscow stopped just twenty seconds after it touched down. Soviet scientists had no idea what happened, but the one photograph they received provided a possible clue. When the spacecraft had arrived on Mars, one of the greatest dust storms ever recorded was raging across the planet. Since the photograph was dark and showed no details, scientists suspected that *Mars 3* had been tipped over by the fierce Martian winds, which caused its radio link to be broken.

Although neither of the Soviet rovers accomplished its intended mission, *Mars 2* (in spite of its crash landing) earned the distinction of being the first human-made object to ever reach the Martian surface. The orbiters fared a little better, both completing their journeys around Mars. They sent back a series of photographs, but because of the dust storm the images were no more discernible than the photo taken by *Mars 3*. The spacecraft were able to take measurements of the planet's temperature, gravity, and magnetic fields, though, and these findings were transmitted back to Moscow.

An American President's Vision

The Soviet Union was highly secretive about its Mars missions, so the details were not known for many years. However, the United States was well aware of the Soviets' aggressive pursuit of space exploration, and that fueled America's interest in its own space program. No one was more enthusiastic about the effort than the country's newly elected president, John F. Kennedy. In a May 25, 1961, speech, Kennedy stressed the need for America to make space exploration a high priority: "Now it is time to take longer strides—time for a great new American enterprise—time for this nation to take a clearly leading role in space achievement, which in many ways may hold the key to our future on earth." To emphasize how serious he was about America's space program, Kennedy asked Congress for funds to develop a rocket that could "someday [provide] a means for even more exciting and ambitious exploration of space, perhaps beyond the moon, perhaps to the very end of the solar system itself."[20]

With the president's official endorsement, NASA enthusiastically began to plan America's future space

Scientists from the former Soviet Union repair a satellite. The Soviets landed the first Martian rover in 1971.

missions. Sheehan describes this renewed zeal for exploring planets millions of miles away: "Scientists saw a chance to hitch their instruments to rockets bound for other worlds, where they could finally learn whether generations of thinkers about the cosmos and man's place in it had been right in supposing there might be other Earth-like worlds in the universe."[21] For many of these scientists, the most compelling reason for exploring other planets in the solar system was the possibility of discovering some form of life. The only two planets where life was likely to exist were Venus and Mars, and because Venus was closest, America would travel there first.

In December 1962, the Venus-bound *Mariner 1* blasted off. However, a seemingly minor computer problem—a stray semicolon in the guidance software—caused the launch vehicle to fail, which sent the spacecraft tumbling into the Atlantic Ocean. Fortunately for NASA, the second spacecraft, *Mariner 2,* launched successfully, exiting Earth's atmosphere and sweeping past Venus, where it took detailed measurements of the planet's temperatures and atmosphere. After scientists analyzed the readings, which showed an atmosphere that was thick and choking and temperatures that were hot enough to melt solid metal, they determined that Venus could not possibly harbor any form of life. So, NASA turned its attention toward Mars. The next opposition would occur in two years, and the United States planned to send two spacecraft millions of miles through space on a journey to the red planet.

Destination: The Red Planet

As the time drew closer for America's first Mars voyage, scientists had high expectations for what the mission would reveal. Most of them hoped some form of life would be found—vegetation, insects, perhaps some species of animals. Some, like astronomer Earl C. Slipher, even clung to the belief that Percival Lowell had been right about the canals. Over the years, Slipher had taken more than one hundred thousand photographs of Mars, which he used to produce a detailed map of the Martian surface. He also discovered a massive dark region that he believed was evidence of vegetation. Slipher died in 1964, so he never saw Mars exploration come to fruition, but his faith in the planet's ability to harbor life lived on in the minds and hearts of many scientists. In fact, it was Slipher's map that was initially used as a chart for U.S. voyages to Mars—and the map clearly showed Lowell's network of canals.

America's first Mars exploration attempt would be a flyby mission. The two spacecraft, *Mariner 3* and *Mariner 4*, carried instruments that would measure the planet's radiation, magnetic fields, and atmospheric pressure, as well as cameras for photographing the Martian surface. To provide power after leaving Earth's atmosphere, each was equipped with thousands of solar cells mounted on four large solar panels. The panels were designed to face the sun during most of the flight, and would collect solar energy and convert it into electrical power.

On November 5, 1964, *Mariner 3*'s launch rocket blasted off on schedule, but just nine hours later the voyage came to an end. A fiberglass nose cone, designed to protect the spacecraft's instruments from the friction of Earth's atmosphere, did not jettison as planned. Instead, the shield remained in place, weighing the spacecraft down and preventing its solar panels from collecting the sun's energy. As a result, its batteries lost power and the mission failed. The second spacecraft was ready to go, but the liftoff had to be postponed. Unless engineers determined what had gone wrong the first time, *Mariner 4* was destined to suffer the same fate as its twin.

Only three weeks remained in the launch window so the situation was urgent, as author Franklin O'Donnell describes:

> The race against the clock had begun and engineers had only one month to get it ready to depart for the red planet. The next few days became what some outside observers hail as JPL crisis engineering at its best. Working with contractors and partners, JPL created what in engineering [jargon] is known as a 'tiger team'—a small, nimble group of its best people with a mission to quickly diagnose and fix a problem.[22]

In just four days, engineers discovered that the problem was a structural defect in the launch vehicle's nose cone, rather than a problem with the spacecraft. Within three weeks they had designed and built a new shield, tested it, and installed it on the rocket that had been waiting on the launch pad in Florida. On November 28, 1964, three weeks after the first launch failed, *Mariner 4* blasted into space and headed toward Mars.

From Elation to Shock
After a seven-month journey, *Mariner 4* reached its Mars orbit on July 14, 1965. The spacecraft's trajectory

Scientists work on a Mariner *spacecraft.* Mariner 4 *reached its Mars orbit in July 1965.*

steered it behind the planet where its radio signals could pass directly through the Martian atmosphere. This had been a conscious decision because it was the best way for the spacecraft to measure the atmosphere's pressure, temperature, and density. However, it was also very risky. For the first part of its orbit *Mariner 4* would be on the dark side of Mars, where its solar panels were not exposed to the sun. During that time, the Martian atmosphere would disrupt radio transmissions, so NASA scientists would lose all contact. If they could not reestablish it, every bit of the spacecraft's data would be lost. After a tense forty-five minutes, *Mariner 4* finally emerged on the sunlit side of Mars and resumed its transmissions to Earth. NASA scientists were elated. For the first time in history, they would see close-up photos of another planet, and even though the Soviets had led the space race until now, these photos would be from an American spacecraft.

When the fuzzy images of the Martian surface finally began to appear, however, the mood at NASA changed from euphoria to stunned silence. For years, Mars and Earth were thought to be very much alike, so scientists expected to see many similarities.

Instead, they stared with disbelief at a planet that was scarred with enormous craters and looked every bit as dead and lifeless as Earth's own moon. Scientific author Robert Godwin describes the reaction at NASA as the photos began to come into focus:

> The 22 grainy black and white pictures returned by Mariner 4 changed mankind's notion of Mars forever. No canals, no ancient cities. . . . For many it was a disillusioning blow that almost killed the romance of the red planet forever. The science fiction writers would be forever forced to revise their Martian fables, no more Barsoom and the beautiful Princesses, no elegant crystal cities or lush jungle landscapes. The masterworks of Burroughs and Bradbury would finally have to be appraised in a different way, as great literary works from a different and more romantic era.[23]

The Exploration Continues

As shocking as *Mariner 4*'s findings were, they did little to diminish scientists' desire to continue with Mars exploration. Most of them still believed that Mars and Earth had been nearly identical when they were formed, and now—even more than before—they wondered what had happened to cause such drastic changes. Also, the spacecraft had been able to photograph only 1 percent of the Martian surface, so it was possible that the rest of the planet was different. NASA intended to find out if this was the case.

In 1969 the United States launched two more Mars probes, hoping that their findings would be more promising. Like their predecessors, *Mariner 6* and *Mariner 7* were flyby spacecraft, but they were heavier and more advanced versions of *Mariner 4*. Each was equipped with two television cameras and scientific instruments that could measure the temperature, pressure, and chemical composition of the Martian atmosphere. Together they sent back two

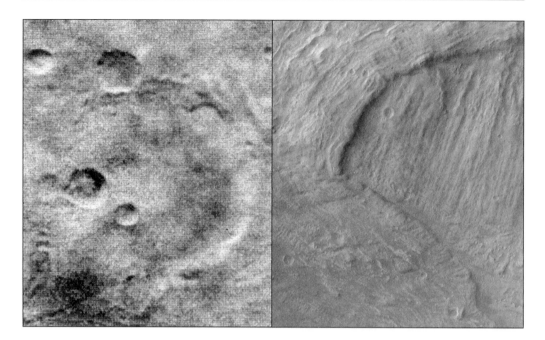

Photographs like these taken by the Mariner *spacecrafts show that the Martian surface is very different from that of Earth.*

hundred photos of Mars, including more than fifty that were taken from only a few thousand miles above the planet's surface. When the photos were displayed on television monitors at JPL headquarters, scientists were able to see about 10 percent of the Martian landscape. Once again, the findings were extremely discouraging because the images showed Mars to be a heavily cratered, bleak, and desolate planet. Also, the spacecraft's instrument readings showed that Mars's atmosphere could not support any form of life. As a result of these new findings, NASA issued a mission report that declared, "The planet Mars is a cold, inhospitable desert."[24]

The next two *Mariner* missions were launched in 1971. Unlike their flyby predecessors, these spacecraft were orbiters capable of mapping the entire Martian surface over a long period of time. Much to NASA's dismay, the first spacecraft, *Mariner 8*, was lost when one of its rockets failed to ignite. However, its twin successfully reached its Mars orbit—but immediately encountered the same sort of fierce dust storm that had likely crippled the Soviet Union's

Mars 3 lander. Blinded by the thick, swirling dust, *Mariner 9*'s cameras were unable to transmit any images for more than a month. Once the dust finally cleared, *Mariner 9* began sending photographs and as scientists studied them, they soon realized they had grossly misjudged Mars. The images clearly showed that only a portion of the planet was heavily cratered and barren, while other areas were covered with diverse geological features. For the first time, close-up photographs revealed details of the immense Valles Marineris and Tharsis Bulge, as well as enormous volcanoes such as Olympus Mons, the north and south polar caps, and winding valleys and channels that looked like they had been carved by ancient rivers or floods. Scientists were also able to see close-up images of the two Martian moons, Phobos and Deimos.

Mariner 9's orbit lasted for a year, and during that time the spacecraft transmitted more than seven thousand photos of Mars. It also provided a vast amount of information about the planet's atmospheric composition, density, pressure, and temperature, as well as data about surface composition, temperature, and gravity. The findings were invaluable, and they enhanced the intrigue of Mars more than any mission had before, as planetary scientist Bruce Murray explains: "Lowell's Earthlike Mars was forever gone, but so was the moonlike Mars portrayed by our first three flyby missions. . . . The Mars revealed by Mariner 9 was not one-dimensional; it was an intriguingly varied planet with a mysterious history. The possibility of early life once more emerged."[25]

Chapter 4

An Era of Discovery

The summer of 1976 marked the beginning of an exciting new dimension in Mars exploration: studying the planet from its surface rather than from above. On July 20, an American spacecraft called *Viking 1* separated from its orbiter, parachuted down, and landed on Mars in an area known as Chryse Planitia. As the lander was programmed to do, it immediately photographed one of its footpads and sent the picture back to mission control. The image showed that the footpad was resting on the surface, rather than buried in deep Martian dust. The spacecraft continued transmitting photos, and as scientists studied them they were ecstatic. For the first time in history, they were staring at close-up color images of the surface of Mars. Carl Sagan, who was part of the *Viking* mission team, described his reaction:

> I remember being transfixed by the first lander image to show the horizon of Mars. This was not an alien world, I thought. I knew places like it in Colorado and Arizona and Nevada. There were rocks and sand drifts and a distant eminence, as natural and unselfconscious as any landscape on Earth. Mars was a place. . . . One way or another, I knew, this was a world to which we would return.[26]

Searching for Martian Life

Viking 1's successful landing was the culmination of more than nine years of planning and development. As with all American Mars missions, two identical spacecraft were sent, but because they were composed of both an orbiter and a lander, these spacecraft were different from any the United States had previously launched. The landers, each encased in a protective pod, sat atop their orbiters. When the spacecraft were fully fueled, each weighed more than six thousand pounds—nearly three times heavier than any spacecraft before them. As a result of this massive weight, the *Viking* journey took ten months, instead of the typical six or seven months for prior Mars missions.

Author and astronomer Carl Sagan (shown here with a Viking *model) was part of the team that sent* Viking 1 *to Mars in July 1976.*

The *Viking* mission had several important goals, one of which was to obtain images of the Martian surface that could answer some questions raised by the *Mariner* photos. The spacecraft would also analyze the atmosphere and make inferences about the planet's interior. But *Viking*'s most important objective, as stated in a NASA mission report, was to search for evidence of living things: "The question of life on Mars has been [speculated on] for a hundred years. There is no conclusive way to determine its existence other than direct search by landing a vehicle on the planet. The Viking mission will do that."[27]

A key factor in the landers' search for life was hunting for water, since scientists knew living things could not survive without it. Both were equipped with cameras that could easily identify anything that moved nearby and instruments designed to scoop up Martian soil. Once soil samples had been obtained, analyzing instruments would test for current organic life, as well as signs that life may have existed in the past. As the landers gathered data, they transmitted it to the orbiters, which in turn sent it back to Earth. Between the orbiters and the landers, any form of life on Mars would surely be found, as NASA scientist Gerald Soffen quips:

> Many of the Viking instruments could have detected life. The orbiter camera could have seen cities or the lights of civilizations. The infrared mapper could have found an unusual heat source from concentration of life forms. The water vapor sensor could have detected watering holes or moisture from some great metabolic source. . . . Seismometers [which measure quake activity] could have detected a nearby elephant.[28]

Exploring from the Surface and the Sky

When the *Viking 1* orbiter reached Mars on June 19, 1976, its first priority was to scout the surface for

suitable landing sites. This was a difficult task, and NASA scientists deliberated for a month to find a place that would be free of large boulders or other dangerous hazards on the ground. Finally, on July 20 the orbiter was given the signal to release its lander, and once the two had separated, the orbiter resumed its own duties in space. Less than two months later the second *Viking* spacecraft *(Viking 2)* arrived. Scientists wanted it to explore a different part of Mars, so the orbiter scouted an area called Utopia, four thousand miles away from the first landing site. When a suitable spot was found, the lander left its mother ship and parachuted down to the surface.

Over the course of their mission, the *Viking* spacecraft provided scientists with a wealth of information. Together, the landers returned more than four thousand photographs, and the orbiters transmitted more than fifty thousand. The spacecraft continued sending data back to Earth until 1982—far longer than the three or four months originally projected. Based on their findings, scientists learned that the Martian soil was composed of iron-rich clay and that the polar caps were at least partially made of water ice with a covering of carbon dioxide. The high concentration of atmospheric CO_2 was discovered, along with the slight traces of oxygen and water vapor, and the atmosphere was confirmed to be much thinner than Earth's. Also, atmospheric ozone was found to be almost nonexistent, which told scientists there was nothing to protect the Martian surface from the sun's deadly ultraviolet rays.

Despite all the *Viking*'s valuable discoveries, however, the mission did not find what NASA had long been hoping for: tangible signs of Martian life. No trace of surface water was found, and the various experiments and analyses failed to confirm any sign of organic molecules or substances, or any indication at all of living things. Some chemical activity was detected in the soil, so most scientists agreed that Martian life could have existed in the past—but only in the past. Yet according to biologist Norman Horowitz, even though the mission dashed all hopes for finding life on Mars, its discoveries were extremely valuable: "It now seems certain that the Earth is the only inhabited planet in the solar system. We have come to the end of the dream. We are alone—we and the other species that share the planet with us. If the Viking findings can make us feel the uniqueness of the Earth and thereby increase our determination to prevent its destruction, they will have contributed more than just science."[29]

Failure and Success

Seventeen years passed before the United States attempted another journey to Mars. The *Viking* mission had cost a staggering $1 billion, and NASA needed to address other priorities such as developing a space shuttle, which consumed the agency's time and budget. Then on September 25, 1992, Mars exploration took off again when an orbiter called *Mars Observer* was launched. Unlike all prior Mars-bound spacecraft, this one made the journey alone, without a companion.

Mars Observer's main goal was to scan the entire Martian surface, taking photographs that were in much finer detail than any taken before. The spacecraft carried a wide array of sophisticated instruments, one of which was designed to measure Mars's magnetic fields. It did not accomplish its mission, however. After traveling for eleven months, *Mars Observer* was lost just three days before it was scheduled to reach Mars. Investigations showed no evidence of a cause, but scientists believed that a clogged fuel line had likely ruptured, crippling the spacecraft and ending all transmissions.

The loss of the orbiter was a tremendous disappointment for NASA scientists. And at a cost of $980 million, it was an expensive failure. Still, the United States remained firm in its commitment to continue exploring Mars. Two years after the mission failed, NASA announced an aggressive exploration plan called the Mars Surveyor Program. Over the following decade, numerous spacecraft would be sent to Mars with the goal of gaining a more in-depth understanding of the red planet and its history. Future voyages would include orbiters as well as orbiter/lander combinations, with each mission more advanced than those before it.

The first of NASA's missions was the *Mars Global Surveyor (MGS)* orbiter, which was launched on November 7, 1996. With an immense amount of computing power and memory, *MGS* was the most powerful spacecraft ever sent to Mars. Yet in spite of its vast capabilities, the orbiter was tiny compared with its predecessor—just twenty-three hundred pounds. Its objective was to learn more about Mars's surface and atmosphere and gain a greater understanding of what had caused such drastic changes over the planet's history. During its orbit, *MGS* was programmed to monitor global climate

The Mars Global Surveyor *studied the Martian surface and atmosphere and monitored global climate changes and weather patterns.*

changes and weather patterns over a long period of time.

The orbiter reached Mars eleven months after launch and began to transmit data back to Earth. As of late 2003, *MGS* had taken more than 150,000 photos of Mars, many of which showed such intricate detail that objects no bigger than a school bus were visible. Among its many discoveries were crescent-shaped dunes and gullies, channels, and other indentations in the planet's surface that suggested the presence of water beneath the ground. It also photographed seasonal climate changes and weather-related phenomena such as massive, swirling storms of fine red dust.

One of the scientific instruments aboard *MGS* was a laser altimeter (an instrument that measures elevation), which gave scientists their first three-dimensional view of Mars's polar ice caps. Another instrument called a magnetometer was designed to measure the planet's magnetic field. As the spacecraft swooped within seventy miles of the surface, the instrument recorded peculiar pockets of magnetism in the most ancient Martian terrain. From this, scientists inferred that Mars once had a magnetic field; as the planet changed over time, remnants of the magnetism were preserved in fossilized rocks.

Mars Global Surveyor's mission was scheduled to last four years, but its longevity far exceeded scientists' expectations. As of 2004 the spacecraft was still transmitting data, and over the course of its orbit, *MGS* collected more information about Mars than all previous missions combined.

A One-Ton Beach Ball

At the same time *MGS* was being developed, another Mars mission was in the works. Since the time of the *Viking* mission, the United States had not sent a lander to explore the Martian surface. NASA scientists wanted to resume the exploration, but they needed a solution that was more affordable than the *Viking* mission. Their answer was *Pathfinder*, a relatively low-cost spacecraft that would leave Earth via a launch vehicle, spiral millions of miles through space, and land on Mars without a companion to assist with the landing. *Pathfinder* would not make the voyage alone, however. A tiny roving robot named *Sojourner* was traveling along, and once the spacecraft had safely landed on Mars, the rover would set out on its own to explore the surface. The mission had both technological and scientific goals: to prove that relatively low-cost spacecraft could successfully land on their own and to explore the Martian surface and garner valuable data about the planet's history. *Pathfinder*'s success would also pave the way for future Martian exploration, including voyages that carried humans.

Figuring out how to land *Pathfinder* was the biggest challenge faced by NASA scientists. Without an orbiter to scout the surface, the right landing site had to be determined ahead of time. After screaming through space at sixteen thousand miles per hour, the lander would open a huge, billowing parachute and fire several retro-rockets to slow its descent through the Martian atmosphere. But even then, the two-thousand-pound craft would hit the surface at speeds of fifty to one hundred miles per hour. Something was needed to cushion the impact, and scientists decided to expand on technology used in automobiles: an air bag system that would inflate just before landing. Because the Martian terrain was known to be extremely rough, the air bags had to be strong enough to resist tearing or puncturing if the spacecraft landed on jagged rocks or boulders.

Scientists prepare the Sojourner *roving robot (circled) for its mission to Mars.*

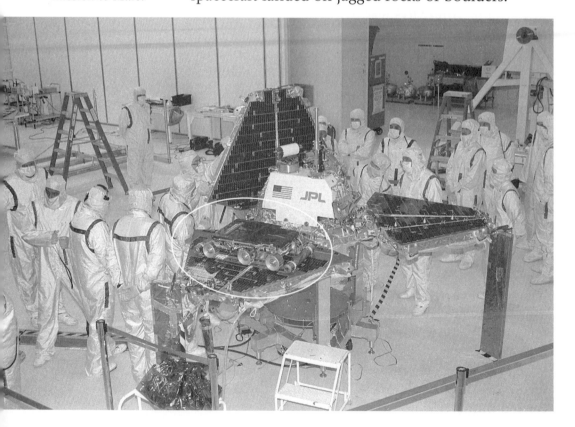

On December 4, 1996, *Pathfinder* blasted off and headed for Mars. Exactly seven months later, on the Fourth of July, it passed through the Martian atmosphere, shed its heat shield, and unfurled its enormous parachute. Ten seconds before it slammed into the surface, a massive cluster of air bags inflated and encased the lander in a protective cocoon. Like an enormous rubber ball, *Pathfinder* dropped to the ground and bounced about fifty feet into the air. After fifteen to twenty more bounces, the lander rolled around the surface and then finally came to a stop. When it transmitted an "A-OK" signal back to JPL headquarters, the packed control room erupted into applause, cheers, and tears over an event that was both incredible and historic.

Roaming the Surface

Once the air bags had deflated, *Pathfinder*'s three panels opened up like the petals of a flower and its camera began to take pictures. Scientists could see dark rocks, red dust, a pale yellow Martian sky—and the deflated air bags billowing out around the lander instead of retracting. With its off-ramps blocked, *Sojourner* was stuck on the lander and could not roll off. Ground engineers fixed the problem by directing one of the panels to open further, which allowed the air bags to fully retract. By the end of the second day (or sol, as a Martian day is known), *Pathfinder*'s camera was transmitting images that showed *Sojourner* rolling down the ramp and making its first tracks in the Martian soil, with ground controllers using remote control to "drive" it from Earth.

The tiny *Sojourner* was no bigger than a microwave oven and weighed just twenty-three pounds, but NASA scientist Ricaurte Chock describes it as the real star of the show: "This is the first time that anybody has operated a wheeled vehicle on another planet, and I'm pleased to tell you that it set a world speed record for the fastest vehicle ever to go on the world of Mars. The speed record was . . . about one-fiftieth of a mile per hour—but that is faster than anybody has ever gone on Mars before."[30] As *Sojourner* wheeled along the surface, it used tiny cameras to take photos of rocks that scientists whimsically named Yogi, Boo Boo, Stimpy, Froggy, Ratbert, Barnacle Bill, Marvin the Martian, and Snukums, among others. Using an X-ray spectrometer, the rover analyzed rocks and soil to determine their chemical properties and found that the darker rocks appeared to have a high amount of a hard, glassy mineral known as silica, while the lighter ones were rich in sulfur. Also, there were rocks of varied textures, as well as rounded cobbles (rock fragments), that hinted at a warmer and wetter past.

While *Sojourner* focused on the Martian surface, the lander used its built-in weather station to study climate and weather patterns. It found that ice clouds were common in the morning and then dissipated in the afternoon, and surface temperatures changed abruptly between day and night. *Pathfinder* also confirmed that dust absorbed solar radiation in the Martian atmosphere, which partially blocked solar energy from reaching the surface.

By the time the *Pathfinder* mission was over, the two spacecraft had transmitted 16,500 photos of the Martian surface and 8.5 million measurements of the planet's temperature and atmospheric pressure. Their longevity also far exceeded scientists' expectations; the lander operated nearly three times longer than expected and the rover operated twelve times longer than the projected seven days. The end eventually came, however. On September 27, 1997, ground engineers received the last transmission. Both spacecraft had functioned far longer than anyone dreamed they would, yet scientists felt a great sense of loss when the mission was over. Raeburn says *Pathfinder* was one of the most successful missions in history: "America's space exploration pro-

gram was back on track. Mars had become a friend-
lier and more familiar place." And the future of Mars
exploration was brighter than ever.[31]

From Disappointment to Triumph

In addition to its many valuable discoveries,
Pathfinder had proven something profound: Spacecraft could journey to Mars on their own, land
safely, and accumulate a wealth of information as
they explored the planet's surface. With anticipation
of continued success, NASA scientists prepared for
the next launch opportunity in 1999.

On January 3, a spacecraft called *Mars Polar Lander*
blasted off, carrying two instruments called probes.
Just before the lander entered the Martian atmosphere, the probes would fall to the surface and
deeply penetrate the ground. Then they would start
transmitting information to *Mars Global Surveyor*,
which would send the data back to Earth. After the
lander had touched down, it would scoop up soil

Sojourner *rolls across
the Martian surface.
The* Pathfinder
*mission proved to be
one of the most
successful in history.*

samples and analyze them and record Martian sounds on a special microphone. None of these plans came to fruition, though, because the mission failed. Ground controllers lost all contact with the spacecraft just as it entered the Martian atmosphere; it was later assumed that faulty computer software had caused it to crash while attempting to land.

Although the loss of *Mars Polar Lander* was a huge setback for NASA, officials viewed it as a wake-up call: In an effort to cut costs, they had not spent enough time and money on adequate testing. The result was a complete reevaluation of the space exploration program, as well as improvements to ensure that such a failure would not happen again. With a firm resolve to press on with Mars exploration, the agency began to plan the next mission: an orbiter named *Mars Odyssey*.

For the first time since the *Viking* mission in 1976, this voyage would involve both orbiting and landing spacecraft. NASA scientist Bob Mase explains why:

> Before you send any landers to Mars, you want to look at the planet as a whole. We call that "global reconnaissance." . . . Orbiters can't scrape rocks and look at them microscopically, and rovers cannot traverse and image the entire planet. So, the two types of missions really complement one another. It's difficult to communicate from the surface of Mars directly to Earth. You'd need a big antenna and a lot of power. It turns out that the rovers can more efficiently send the information up to the orbiters, which are better equipped to relay the data back to Earth.[32]

Mars Odyssey was launched in April 2001 and reached Mars the following October. Its function was to survey the entire Martian surface during its orbit and to be a communication vehicle for the *Mars Exploration Rover (MER)* mission scheduled for launch

Navigation Cameras

Panoramic Camera

Panoramic Camera

Mini–thermal Emission Spectrometer
at rear

Low-gain Antenna

High-gain
Antenna

Magnet Array
collects dust for analysis

Solar Arrays

Rocker-bogie
Mobility System

Microscopic
Camera

Mars Exploration Rover (MER)

Rock
Abrasion Tool

Moessbauer
Spectrometer

Alpha Particle
X-ray Spectrometer

in 2003. Two identical spacecraft would be sent on the *MER* voyage, each carrying a lander with a rover encased inside. Unlike *Pathfinder*, these landers would carry no scientific instruments; their only purpose was to ensure that the rovers were delivered safely to the Martian surface. Within a few days after touchdown, the two rovers would leave their landers behind and drive off to explore the planet.

On June 10, 2003, the first *MER* spacecraft blasted off on its way to Mars, carrying a rover named *Spirit*. Four weeks later its twin took off, accompanied by a rover named *Opportunity*. After traveling for seven months, the spacecraft reached Mars three weeks apart and landed in much the same way as *Pathfinder:* Parachutes deployed, retro-rockets fired, a massive cluster of air bags inflated, and the landers bounced like giant rubber balls upon the Martian ground before finally rolling to a stop. Then the air bags deflated and retracted, the landers' petals opened up, and *Spirit* and *Opportunity* were released from their protective housing. After seven years, America was back on the surface of Mars.

Robot Geologists

Spirit and *Opportunity* landed on opposite sides of the planet. Scientists chose their landing sites based on where they believed there was once liquid water. The rovers' mission was to search for and study many different types of rocks and soil that might hold clues to past water activity, including searching for minerals that would not have formed unless water had been present. Unlike in past missions, these rovers would not be searching for life but for clues to an environment that may have supported life in the past.

Once they were on the Martian surface, *Spirit* and *Opportunity* resembled strange galactic creatures. Each weighed four hundred pounds and was about the size of a riding lawn mower, with a flat-topped equipment deck, six motorized wheels, and a rotating mast assembly that served as the "head and neck." Winglike solar panels provided power for up to four hours per sol, and two rechargeable batteries furnished back-up power when the sun was not shining.

To perform their experiments, both rovers were outfitted with instruments that allowed them to function as robotic geologists. Their masts were capable of rotating 360 degrees, and small panoramic cameras mounted on top of the masts would capture high-quality close-up images of the surface. Three more pairs of cameras located on the front, back, and mast of each rover enabled them to see their surroundings and navigate around obstacles. In addition, each rover had a robotic arm that could bend and move much the same way as a human arm: with a shoulder, elbow, and wrist. Attached to the arm was a magnifying camera that allowed scientists to examine the fine structure of rocks and soil; also attached was a drill called a Rock Abrasion Tool (RAT) that was designed to grind away the outer surfaces of rocks so that the interiors could be exposed for examination. Powerful antennas located on each rover's equipment deck served as both their voice and ears, facilitating two-way communication with Earth and with orbiters in the sky above them.

Amazing Success

From the very first day that *Spirit* and *Opportunity* started roaming around the Martian surface, scientists at mission control were thrilled with their discoveries. *Opportunity* dug into the rocks in the enormous Eagle Crater, while *Spirit* focused on a large rock named "Humphrey." Collectively, they proved what scientists had long suspected: There was no question that Mars was once soaked with water, including the likelihood that there were once saltwater seas. The rovers found evidence of sulfates and other

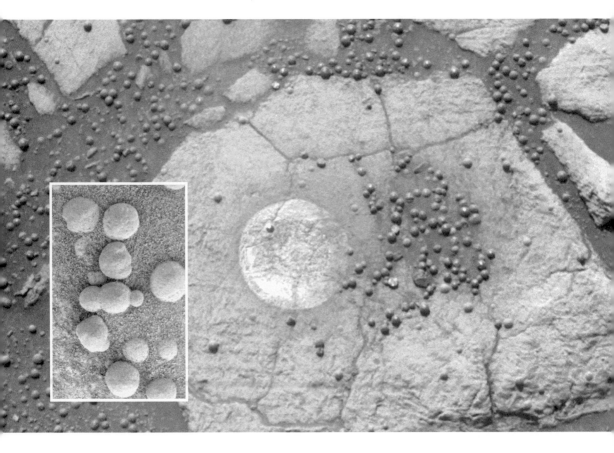

Scientists contend that these small Martian rock formations, called blueberries, must have been formed by water.

minerals, including a rare mineral known as jarosite, that could have formed only if water had existed on the planet long ago. Plus, they discovered geological formations called "blueberries"—small globular-shaped depressions in rocks that had to have been formed by water. Once the initial examinations were complete, *Spirit* and *Opportunity* drove on to study other rock formations and craters. One crater examined by *Opportunity* was as large as a football stadium. *Spirit*, meanwhile, dug into a range of hills named Columbia Hills in memory of the astronauts who died on the *Columbia* space shuttle. Together, the two rovers returned thousands of color photographs, as well as invaluable scientific data.

Spirit and *Opportunity* were originally scheduled to explore Mars for three months. However, in April

2004 the rovers were operating well enough for the mission to be extended for at least five more months. According to Matt Wallace, JPL mission manager, it is hard to predict when the two rovers will actually quit working, but of course, he and other scientists must be prepared for that. As for how they will handle it, Wallace says they just have to step back and say, "Hey, this is a machine. That's why we send machines to these hazardous environments before we send humans. . . . But it's always tough at the end . . . no matter how it comes or when it comes."[33]

Chapter 5

Mars in the Future

"The planet Mars," writes Robert Zubrin, "is a world of breathtaking scenery, with spectacular mountains three times as tall as Mount Everest, canyons three times as deep and five times as long as the Grand Canyon, vast ice fields, and thousands of kilometers of mysterious dry riverbeds. Its unexplored surface may hold unimagined riches and resources for future humanity, as well as answers to some of the deepest philosophical questions that thinking

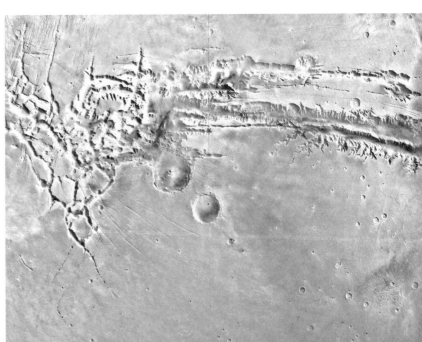

men and women have pondered for millennia. . . . But all that Mars holds will forever remain beyond our grasp unless and until men and women walk its rugged landscapes."[34]

In one paragraph, Zubrin explains why human exploration of Mars is such an important aspect of any future space exploration. Only humans have the ability to see, feel, and touch the red planet, ponder their surroundings, and draw conclusions based on their discoveries. Though it is true that scientists have gained a wealth of knowledge from space missions, until human beings can travel to Mars and explore it for themselves, many of its mysteries will forever remain unsolved.

Futuristic Views

Many years before any spacecraft paid a visit to Mars, scientists were thinking about the possibilities of human exploration. One such scientist was the late Wernher von Braun, a rocket designer who left his native Germany and moved to the United States

A Viking *photograph shows one of the vast, deep canyons that makes up the Martian landscape.*

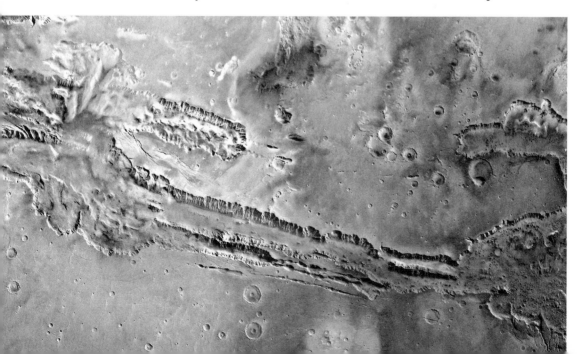

after World War II. Von Braun was convinced that a manned Mars mission was not only essential but achievable. During the late 1940s and 1950s, he often spoke publicly about his enthusiasm for sending people to Mars, and even took it upon himself to plan such an expedition in great detail. In his book *The Mars Project*, von Braun stressed that an entire fleet of spaceships would be needed for the journey, as former NASA information specialist Annie Platoff explains: "[Von Braun wrote] that if [Christopher] Columbus had sailed with only one ship rather than a fleet of three ships he might never have made it

German rocket designer Wernher von Braun believed that a manned mission to Mars was both possible and essential.

back to Spain with news of his discoveries. 'So it is with interplanetary exploration: it must be done on a grand scale.'"[35] Von Braun's reference to "grand scale" was apparent in his description of the spacecraft that were needed for the journey. He envisioned a fleet of ten vessels that would carry a minimum of seventy people to Mars. Seven spacecraft would serve as passenger carriers, while the other three would transport cargo, including winged landers that would carry the crew down to the surface.

During the 1950s, von Braun wrote a series of articles for a popular magazine called *Collier's*. He told of his ambitious plans for Mars exploration, but he also cautioned that because of all the unknowns, the journey would not be possible for nearly a century. By the end of ten years, however, he had formed an entirely different conclusion. In an article written for a November 1965 issue of *Astronautics & Aeronautics*, von Braun stated that a manned mission to Mars would be possible by the year 1982, and he urged that such a mission be considered a high priority:

> You will have gathered from my paper here that I am an optimist with respect to our space program. However, even if those pessimists should prevail with their gloomy predictions that science has brought mankind close to the abyss, and that it's only a short time before man will blow himself up on this planet, let me suggest that even that seems to indicate that we should pursue this course of going to Mars. In fact, we should indeed hurry, so that we can establish a foothold on a new planet as long as we have one left to take off from.[36]

In 1969 von Braun made a formal presentation to NASA in which he explained in great detail his plans for a human expedition to Mars. He was highly regarded by government officials because of his role in developing the *Saturn V*, an enormous rocket that launched the crew of America's first mission to the moon. In his Mars presentation, von Braun expressed his belief that "the next frontier is manned exploration of the planets."[37] Of course, 1982 came and went and no humans set foot on Mars. But according to Platoff, von Braun's theories were inspiring to scientists, and his work was a major influence on NASA's overall long-term plan for human interplanetary missions: "Basic elements of von Braun's Mars Project—such as the use of reusable shuttle-like ferry vessels, orbital assembly, and multiple spacecraft to reach Mars—continued to show up in proposals for human journeys to the Red Planet."[38]

Human Explorers Versus Robots

Even though von Braun died in 1977, his passion and enthusiasm for human Mars exploration is still very much alive today. Aside from the excitement of such a mission, the main reason scientists feel strongly about sending humans to Mars is rather simple: People have capabilities that machines do not. Even with today's advanced technology, there are limitations to what robots can do, and robots rely solely on people to think for them by providing precise, detailed instructions. For instance, the *Spirit* and *Opportunity* rovers have mechanical arms to lift rocks and soil off the ground, instruments to analyze the material, and cameras to take high-quality photographs. But they cannot actually see or feel what they have found or make judgments about it. They do not have human intelligence, intuition, or reasoning ability, nor do they have life experience that could help them make decisions or form conclusions. If their surroundings quickly change, they are at the mercy of people to tell them how to adapt to the changes so they can survive. Those qualities and abilities are inherently human.

Since the time of *Viking 1* and *2*, searching for Martian life (past or present) has been a priority of nearly every mission. This is especially true in light of recent discoveries that water was once abundant on the red planet, because the probability of finding past or present organic life is now greater than ever. That search for life could be performed infinitely better by humans than by robots, as Zubrin explains:

> Since it is unlikely that there is life today on the Martian surface, the search for Martian biology will largely be a search for fossils. Small robotic rovers with their limited range and long communication time delay . . . are a very poor tool for conducting such a search. . . . Fossil searches require mobility, agility, and the ability to use intuition to immediately follow up very subtle clues. Human investigators—rock hounds—are required. If Mars is to be made to give up its secrets, "people who do not shrink from the dreary vastness of space" will have to go there themselves.[39]

Scientists do not necessarily agree on how or when a manned mission to Mars should occur, but most agree that many questions, including the question about Martian life, can be answered only when human beings can explore the red planet. Plus, according to scientist Michael Duke, humans could do the work in a fraction of the time that it takes robots. Even though manned voyages to Mars would take longer to plan and implement than today's robotic missions, Duke says much more scientific work would be accomplished in less time: "Humans could do the same science on Mars in one or two years as robots could do in 100 to 200 years."[40]

A Long and Risky Voyage

Human astronauts who take the bold step of traveling on the very first Mars expedition will not be blind to the risks involved. Long before they board the spacecraft, they will know what to expect—and they will also know there is a chance that they might never return to Earth. In a report for NASA, authors Stephen Hoffman and David Kaplan make this uncertainty very clear:

> The human exploration of Mars will be a complex undertaking. It is an enterprise that will confirm the potential for humans to leave our home planet and make our way outward into the cosmos. Though just a small step on a cosmic scale, it will be a significant one for humans, because it will require leaving Earth with very limited return capability. The commitment to launch is a commitment to several years away from Earth, and there is a very narrow window within which return is possible.[41]

Currently, there is no exact date when a crewed mission will be sent to Mars. However, in a speech given in January 2004, President George W. Bush announced additional financial support for NASA to prepare for future journeys, which would include sending humans back to the moon by 2020 as the first step toward exploring other planets: "The moon is a logical step toward further progress and achievement. With the experience and knowledge gained on the moon, we will then be ready to take the next steps of space exploration: human missions to Mars and to worlds beyond. . . . We do not know where this journey will end. Yet we know this: Human beings are headed into the cosmos."[42]

Most experts say a manned Mars mission could likely occur by the year 2025, but before that can happen, many hurdles must be overcome. A spacecraft would need to carry people, gear, food, and machinery, which means it would be about thirty times heavier than any spacecraft developed for previous missions. Landing such a craft would be a daunting challenge: Bouncing as high as a five-story building would not work quite as well for humans as for ro-

Future Mars Missions

Spacecraft (Mission Type)	Projected Launch	Engineered by	Major Equipment/Goals
Mars Reconnaissance Orbiter (Orbiting satellite)	August 10, 2005	NASA/Jet Propulsion Laboratory/Italian space agency	MRO will have a high resolution stereo camera for close-up photographs of Mars's surface, and a radar sounder to search for subsurface water. The satellite will also help send messages to Earth from future visiting spacecraft.
Phoenix (Robotic lander)	August 2007	NASA/University of Arizona, Tucson	Phoenix will land on Mars's northern pole, dig into the icy soil, then melt and analyze the water ice. It will also scan the Martian atmosphere.
NetLanders (Orbiter and four identical lander stations)	2007	CNES (French space agency) and FMI (Finnish Meteorological Institute)	Simultaneous, multisite experiments will use ground-penetrating radar, magnometers, seismometers, and atmospheric sensors (temperature, humidity, wind, and more).
Mars Science Laboratory (Robotic lander/ rover)	2009 (no exact launch date set)	NASA	This long-term, long-range mobile science laboratory will travel on Mars's surface for at least one year.
Unnamed Spacecraft (Lander/sample return)	2014 (no exact launch date set)	NASA, with French and Italian space agencies (and other international assistance)	A lander will use advanced technology to collect rock and soil samples and then return them to Earth for in-depth analysis.

bots. Another consideration is determining a suitable landing site on the Martian surface where people could "set up camp." Because Mars has a total surface area of more than 200 million square miles, astronauts will be able to explore only a fraction of it. If a spaceship should inadvertently land in a bleak, desolate area thousands of miles from regions worth exploring, the entire mission could be wasted.

One of the greatest risks of a human expedition to Mars is the voyage itself, which would be extremely trying for astronauts. The journey would last six months or longer, and for most of that time they would experience microgravity, or the feeling of weightlessness. Though floating on air may look like fun, it can cause serious physical problems. On past space voyages, astronauts have suffered from disorientation, dizziness, congestion, headaches, and nausea. Someone exposed to microgravity over a much longer period of time could develop more severe ailments, including weak and brittle bones from loss of bone mass, atrophied muscles, kidney stones, and other serious physical problems. Scientists are studying ways to counter the effects of weightlessness, such as providing a source of artificial gravity or providing ways for astronauts to exercise during the journey. At this time, however, microgravity still poses one of the greatest risks for long-distance space travel.

Another danger of such a lengthy voyage is the trillions of micrometeorites shooting through the solar system. These fiery fragments of comets and asteroids may be as tiny as a grain of sand or as large as a golf ball, and they are constantly flying through space from every direction at speeds of over a hundred thousand miles per hour. A Mars-bound spacecraft would likely be pummeled by micrometeorites throughout much of its journey, which could lead to serious damage. Equally dangerous in deep space are the high levels of radiation caused by solar flares and galactic cosmic rays. Unlike on Earth, where the magnetic field forms a protective bubble against radiation, no such protection exists in space. Just as a spacecraft must be strong enough to stand up against micrometeorites, it must also have some kind of shield that can absorb or block as much radiation as possible. If this radiation penetrates a spacecraft, not only can it damage or destroy the vehicle and its instruments, but it can also be deadly to the astronauts.

Dangers of the Red Planet

Assuming the astronauts aboard a Mars-bound spacecraft can survive the perilous six-month journey, the risks they have endured along the way will drop considerably once they arrive at their destination. They may encounter some micrometeorites on the ground, but they will not be bombarded by the objects flying at them from every which way. Also, even though Martian radiation levels are higher than Earth's, the planet itself serves as a shield against the extreme radiation found in deep space. The astronauts will still feel the effects of Mars's low gravity because it is so much weaker than Earth's, but they will no longer have to endure weightlessness. However, there are still many new risks that await astronauts who step outside their spacecraft for the first time. They will experience hostile conditions that no human has ever faced before—and the proper space suit is the only thing that will save their lives.

One of the biggest risks for humans visiting Mars is the planet's low-pressure atmosphere. Air pressure keeps blood and body fluids liquid and flowing. When it is too low, the fluids in a person's body can boil, lose heat quickly, and then evaporate, which can lead to rapid death. David Akin, a professor at the University of Maryland's Space System Laboratory, describes a simulated experience: "I remember hearing a NASA astronaut talk about an experiment in which he was exposed to a sudden, temporary loss of pressure. He said the first thing he thought was, 'Oh ———!' Then he had this interesting feeling of saliva boiling on his tongue. Then he passed out."[43] In order to protect astronauts from the perilous low-pressure atmosphere, space suits must be pressurized. Specialized breathing apparatuses must also be worn because the Martian atmosphere contains extremely high levels of carbon dioxide and only the slightest traces of oxygen and nitrogen.

If astronauts were to breathe the Martian air, they could lose consciousness in as little as fifteen seconds and die shortly thereafter.

The extreme climate and weather conditions found on Mars pose another hazard. Because the Martian climate is extremely cold, space suits would have to be heated. Maintaining comfortable body temperatures is difficult, though, because it can be one temperature at the surface of Mars and twenty or thirty degrees cooler only five feet above it. If a space suit is not designed with that in mind, an astronaut's upper body could be freezing while his or her legs were roasting. In addition, Mars is extremely dusty, and the fine silt hovers in the atmosphere. No one knows for sure whether the dust is toxic, but sci-

An artist's rendering shows some of the equipment that would be necessary for a manned mission to Mars.

entists believe it is a definite possibility. At the very least, it could interfere with the astronauts' ability to see and breathe, so space suits must be designed to protect them from it. This becomes especially important if they were to encounter one of the fierce Martian dust storms, during which hundred-mile-per-hour winds can send dust swirling through the atmosphere for weeks at a time.

Developing space suits for a Mars expedition is a complicated, lengthy process that would take many years. Joe Kosmo, a NASA engineer who designs space suits, says that, unlike astronauts on prior space missions, those who visit Mars will likely spend several years living and working there. That would rule out the bulky attire worn by astronauts on shuttle missions. Even with Mars's low gravity, shuttle space suits would still weigh more than a hundred pounds, and the astronauts wearing them would quickly become exhausted. The ideal space suit will provide the protection astronauts need yet be lightweight enough to be comfortable when worn for long periods of time, as NASA's Phil West explains: "We know how to make a suit you could live in on Mars, but not one that can be effectively manipulated to do jobs there. Such a suit would have to have extremely flexible joints and mix-and-match parts for easy replacement. It would be relatively lightweight, maybe 30 to 40 pounds, but extremely reliable because it would be used for dozens of missions."[44] Even though that suit does not currently exist, Kosmo says the right technologies and materials do exist—now it is just a matter of determining exactly how the suit needs to perform while it is being worn. "The first astronauts on Mars are going to behave like geologists," says Kosmo. "They'll be looking for evidence of life, of water. They'll be poking around, getting down on their hands and knees to look at rocks or drill for samples. They're going to need a really robust suit."[45] NASA is in the process of testing several different models, but until one meets all the necessary criteria, a human expedition to Mars will have to wait.

Mars Direct

Sometime in the distant future, it may be possible for travelers to hop into supersonic spaceships, zoom off to Mars for a week's vacation, and then fly back to Earth, but right now that scenario is found only in science-fiction books. When astronauts finally do make the journey to Mars, they can expect to be away from home for two or three years. With such an extended visit to the red planet, they cannot possibly take enough food, supplies, water, fuel, and equipment with them. Instead, they will have to live off the land, much like the early settlers did during frontier days. Robert Zubrin believes wholeheartedly in that idea:

> Living off the land—intelligent use of local re-
> sources—is not just the way the West was won;
> it's the way the Earth was won, and it's also the
> way Mars can be won. . . . It should come as no
> surprise that local resources make such a differ-
> ence in developing a mission to Mars, or any-
> where else for that matter. Consider what would
> have happened if [American explorers] Lewis
> and Clark had decided to bring all the food, wa-
> ter, and fodder needed for their transcontinen-
> tal journey. Hundreds of wagons would have
> been required to carry the supplies. Those sup-
> ply wagons would need hundreds of horses and
> drivers. A logistics nightmare would have been
> created that would have sent the costs of the ex-
> pedition beyond the resources of the America of
> [Thomas] Jefferson's time.[46]

Zubrin's belief in the importance of human Mars exploration inspired him to create his own mission plan called Mars Direct. Based on his "intelligent use

Robert Zubrin's Mars Direct mission plan (pictured) was inspired by his belief in the importance of human exploration of Mars.

of local resources" philosophy, Zubrin's program features a crewed Mars mission that would be simpler, cheaper, and more successful than traditional mission plans. A crew of astronauts would make the six-month journey to Mars, where they would stay for about a year and a half. Two landers would make the trip: One shaped like a gigantic tuna fish can would transport the astronauts to Mars and serve as their home during the trip, and a second spacecraft would bring them back to Earth. With the help of computerized robots, the astronauts would recycle oxygen and water and make their own fuel by combining ingredients brought from Earth with CO_2 in the Martian atmosphere. Future missions, according to Zubrin's plan, would expand on the first, with more explorers traveling to Mars, living off the land, building greenhouses to grow food, and eventually creating a thriving Martian colony.

First Things First

Some scientists dismiss Zubrin's plan as too simplistic or far-fetched, although most agree that making use of Martian resources is an excellent idea. That is

A scientist tests a robot used to gather information that might help NASA one day send people to Mars.

especially true for creating fuel from the Martian atmosphere, which could shave millions of dollars off a mission's cost. But no matter what the details of the first human Mars expedition, there are still too many unknowns and risks to embark on it in the very near future. Until it is deemed safe to send humans traveling through space on their way to the red planet, Mars exploration will have to be performed by robots. And along with making valuable discoveries, the robots can actually pave the way for human exploration.

According to NASA scientist Doug Ming, robots will be invaluable in answering complicated questions before humans ever set foot on Mars. They can determine where the ground is strong enough to support the landing of spacecraft and identify the best locations to construct buildings.

A scientist tests a robot used to gather information that might help NASA one day send people to Mars.

Robots can also teach humans how to survive in the harsh Martian environment, including searching for subsurface water ice that humans could drill and extract. For example, one of the rover *Spirit*'s tasks is to search for water that is bound in Martian soils and rocks. Ming explains why this is important: "Water bound up in the soil and rocks could be extracted by astronauts to use as nourishment for themselves or fuel for their machines."[47]

Ming says that everything scientists learn from current robotic missions can help immensely in planning future Mars travel that involves humans:

> Space navigators still incorporate sky charts drawn by Babylonian star gazers to send spacecraft on a perfect trajectory to Mars today. Humans going to Mars—soon or even thousands of years from now—will depend on what we learn from our current robotic missions to create the right spacesuits, habitats, and roving vehicles humans will someday drive on Mars. Robots will probably even deliver our first building materials to Mars, so when humans first land, robots will have paved the way for us in more ways than one.[48]

Other space missions in the planning phases will also pave the way toward human Mars exploration. For instance, America's *Mars Reconnaissance Orbiter*, scheduled for launch in August 2005, will scour the Martian surface for water and photograph rocks and other objects as small as a beach ball. This close-up view will enable the spacecraft to search for suitable landing sites for future sample-return missions, considered to be the most exciting and scientifically rewarding Mars explorations ever attempted. Both the European Space Agency and NASA are planning sample-return missions around 2011, during which a robotic spacecraft will travel to Mars, collect soil and rock samples, and return the samples to Earth for analysis. This type of mission will provide scientists with their first hands-on opportunity to study Martian surface material, and will allow them to test a spacecraft's ability to leave Mars and make the long journey back to Earth.

The Future Beckons

No one knows for sure when humans will make the first voyage to Mars, but the time will definitely come when they do. And when that happens, it will be the magical realization of a dream that has survived for centuries, as Paul Raeburn writes:

> Thousands of years after the ancients gazed at Mars with fear and fascination, it remains among the most mysterious and intriguing bodies in the heavens. The exploration of the Earth's surface is nearly complete, and Mars represents a new frontier, a dazzling new destination to fire the imaginations of today's explorers. The technology to send a human mission to Mars is now within reach. And it is conceivable that, some time in the twenty-first century, scientists may join science fiction writers in the exploration of Mars, as human beings, for the first time, step onto the cold red dust of the Martian surface.[49]

Notes

Introduction: The Mysterious Red Planet

1. William Sheehan and Stephen James O'Meera, *Mars: The Lure of the Red Planet.* Amherst, NY: Prometheus, 2001, p. 12.

Chapter 1: Early Observations and Beliefs

2. Carl Sagan, *Cosmos.* New York: Wings, 1995, p. 51.
3. Quoted in Sagan, *Cosmos*, p. 60.
4. Isaac Asimov, *Mars: The Red Planet.* New York: Lothrop, Lee & Shepard, 1977, p. 29.
5. Quoted in William Sheehan, *The Planet Mars: A History of Observation and Discovery.* Tucson: University of Arizona Press, 1996, p. 17.
6. Quoted in Paul Karol and David Catling, *Planet Mars Chronology*, 1991. www-mgcm.arc.nasa.gov/mgcm/fun/mars_chro.html.
7. Sallie Baliunas, "Close Encounter," *Tech Central Station*, August 15, 2003. www.techcentralstation.com/081503B.html.
8. Quoted in Kevin Zahnle, "Decline and Fall of the Martian Empire," *Nature*, July 12, 2001. www.stat.rice.edu/~siefert/PubFiles/ZahnleMars.pdf.
9. Robert Zubrin, *The Case for Mars: The Plan to Settle the Red Planet and Why We Must.* New York: Free Press, 1996, p. 27.

Chapter 2: An Earth-Like World

10. Sagan, *Cosmos*, p. 121.
11. Quoted in European Space Agency, "Martian Interior: Volcanism," *Science & Technology*, June 2, 2004. http://sci.esa.int/science-e/www/object/index.cfm?fobjectid=31028&floodylongid=646.
12. Quoted in European Space Agency, "Mars vs Earth," *Science & Technology*, July 7, 2003. http://sci.esa.int/science-e/www/object/index.cfm?fobjectid=31025.
13. Quoted in David J. Craig, "The Air Up There: BU Planetary

93

Scientist Tracks *Spirit*'s Trip to Mars," *BU Bridge*, January 16, 2004. www.bu.edu/bridge/archive/2004/01-16/mars.html.

14. Space Telescope Science Institute, "Mars' Chaotic Climate," *HubbleSite NewsCenter*, May 20, 1997. http://hubblesite.org/ newscenter/newsdesk/archive/releases/1997/15/astrofile.

15. Quoted in Tony Phillips, "Planet Gobbling Dust Storms," Science@NASA, July 16, 2001. http://science.nasa.gov/head lines/y2001/ast16jul%;5F1.htm.

16. Zubrin, *The Case for Mars*, p. 35.

Chapter 3: The Space Race

17. Quoted in David P. Stern, "Robert Goddard and His Rockets," in *From Stargazers to Starships*, 2001. http://pwg. gsfc.nasa.gov/stargaze.

18. Paul Raeburn, *Uncovering the Secrets of the Red Planet*. Washington, DC: National Geographic Society, 1998, p. 47.

19. Ron Koczor, interview with author, April 29, 2004.

20. John F. Kennedy, "Special Message to the Congress on Urgent National Needs," May 25, 1961, John F. Kennedy Library and Museum. www.cs.umb.edu/jfklibrary.

21. Sheehan and O'Meara, *Mars*, p. 238.

22. Franklin O'Donnell, *JPL 101*, California Institute of Technology, 2002. www.jpl.nasa.gov.

23. Robert Godwin, ed., *Mars: The NASA Mission Reports*. Burlington, ON: Apogee, 2000, p. 3.

24. Quoted in Godwin, *Mars*, p. 59.

25. Quoted in Raeburn, *Uncovering the Secrets of the Red Planet*, p. 66.

Chapter 4: An Era of Discovery

26. Sagan, *Cosmos*, p. 121.

27. Quoted in Godwin, *Mars*, p. 110.

28. Quoted in Joseph M. Boyce, *The Smithsonian Book of Mars*. Washington, DC, and London: Smithsonian Institution Press, 2002, p. 254.

29. Quoted in Boyce, *The Smithsonian Book of Mars*, p. 257.

30. Ricaurte Chock, "*Pathfinder* Mission and Mars Landing," NASA Glenn Research Center, Photovoltaic and Space Experiments Branch, August 7, 2002. http://powerweb.grc. nasa.gov.

31. Raeburn, *Uncovering the Secrets of the Red Planet*, p. 176.

32. Quoted in JPL, "Anniversary Party for *Odyssey* at Mars," *Mars Exploration Rover Mission*, January 11, 2000. www.jpl.nasa.gov.

33. Quoted in Leonard David, "Mars Rovers in Autumn: A Life-and-Death Drama on the Red Planet," Space.com *SpaceFlight*, May 6, 2004. www.space.com/missionlaunches/rovers_autumn_040506.html.

Chapter 5: Mars in the Future

34. Zubrin, *The Case for Mars*, p. 1.
35. Annie Platoff, *Eyes on the Red Planet: Human Mars Mission Planning, 1952–1970*, NASA Technical Publications, July 2001. http://ston.jsc.nasa.gov/collections/TRS/_techrep/CR-2001-208928.pdf.
36. Wernher von Braun, "The Next 20 Years of Interplanetary Exploration," *Astronautics & Aeronautics*, November 1965, p. 34.
37. Wernher von Braun, "Manned Mars Landing: Presentation to the Space Task Group," August 4, 1969, in Godwin, *Mars*, p. 410.
38. Platoff, *Eyes on the Red Planet*.
39. Zubrin, *The Case for Mars*, p. 44.
40. Quoted in David S.F. Portree, "The New Martian Chronicles," *Astronomy*, August 1997, p. 32.
41. Stephen J. Hoffman and David L. Kaplan, "Human Exploration of Mars: The Reference Mission of the NASA Mars Exploration Study Team," NASA, July 1997. http://exploration.jsc.nasa.gov/marsref/Mars1txt.pdf.
42. George W. Bush, "President Bush Announces New Vision for Space Exploration Program," White House press release, January 14, 2004. www.whitehouse.gov/news/releases/2004/01/20040114-3.html.
43. Quoted in Scott Lafee, "The Mars Collection," *New Scientist*, September 2, 2000, p. 34.
44. Quoted in Lafee, "The Mars Collection," p. 34.
45. Quoted in Lafee, "The Mars Collection," p. 34.
46. Zubrin, *The Case for Mars*, p. 6.
47. Quoted in NASA, "From Robot Geologists to Human Geologists on Mars," *Mars Exploration Rover Mission*, January 13, 2004. http://marsrovers.jpl.nasa.gov/spotlight/spirit/a8_20040113.html.
48. Quoted in NASA, "From Robot Geologists to Human Geologists on Mars."
49. Raeburn, *Uncovering the Secrets of the Red Planet*, p. 42.

Glossary

aphelion: The point in a planet's orbit when it is farthest from the sun.

barchan dunes: Crescent-shaped sand dunes that are common on Mars.

carbon dioxide: A colorless, odorless gas that is the main component of the Martian atmosphere.

constellation: A grouping of stars in the sky that form a pattern and are often named for objects, animals, or mythological figures.

elliptical orbit: A noncircular orbit, or one that is shaped similarly to an oval.

escape velocity: The speed at which an object must travel in order to escape from a planet's gravity.

flyby: A mission technique in which a planet is examined by a spacecraft as it flies past it.

geocentric system: A model of the universe with Earth at the center and all objects moving around it.

heliocentric system: A sun-centered model of the universe.

iron oxide: A compound consisting of iron and oxygen, commonly called rust.

jettison: To discard unneeded parts of a spacecraft.

launch vehicle: The rocket used to propel a spacecraft into orbit.

launch window: A range of dates during which a spacecraft can most efficiently be launched for a mission.

magnetometer: An instrument used to measure the direction and/or intensity of magnetic fields.

microgravity: A state in which the gravity is reduced to extremely low levels, such as during space flight.

micrometeorite: A tiny fragment of a meteorite; when seen from Earth, these are often called shooting stars (although they are not stars at all).

moment of inertia: A gauge of how a planet's rotation on its axis is influenced by the distribution of mass inside it.

multistage rocket: A rocket composed of two or more rockets that fire at different times, as additional power is needed.

opposition: The point in a planet's orbit when it is on the opposite side of Earth from the sun.

payload: The cargo, instruments, or equipment carried on exploratory missions by a spacecraft.

perihelion: The point in a planet's orbit when it is closest to the sun.

permafrost: A permanently frozen layer of soil at variable depths below the surface.

plate tectonics: A widely accepted scientific theory that Earth's surface is divided into large, thick plates that are constantly moving and crunching against one another.

probe: Any instrument (such as a spacecraft) used to explore an unknown environment and gather information about it.

retrograde motion: A perceived backward drift of a planet resulting from the forward motion of Earth as it passes the planet.

seismology: The study of earthquakes and the movements and vibrations caused by them.

shield volcano: A volcano that has been formed by smoothly flowing lava, rather than volcanic eruptions; shield volcanoes can grow to towering heights but are gently sloped and often flat on top.

sol: A word used to refer to a Martian day.

solar system: The sun and other celestial bodies within its gravitational influence, including planets, asteroids, moons, comets, and meteors.

terrestrial: Relating to the land, rather than to air or water.

trajectory: The charted course for a spacecraft.

transverse dunes: Ridge-shaped sand dunes that are common on Mars.

For Further Reading

Books

Graham Hancock, *The Mars Mystery*. New York: Three Rivers, 1999. An informative book that examines evidence suggesting that Mars was once home to a lush environment of flowing rivers, lakes, and oceans.

William K. Hartmann, *A Traveler's Guide to Mars*. New York: Workman, 2003. A fascinating book that makes readers feel as though they are paying a personal visit to the red planet.

Sally Ride and Tam O'Shaughnessy, *The Mystery of Mars*. New York: Crown, 1999. Discusses the human fascination with Mars and draws comparisons between the red planet and Earth by discussing evolution, geology, and geography.

Susi Trautmann Wunsch, *The Adventures of* Sojourner*: The Mission to Mars That Thrilled the World*. New York: Mikaya, 1998. An enlightening and informative book about the Mars *Pathfinder* mission and the tiny rover named *Sojourner*.

Periodicals

Mona Chiang, "So, You Want to Go to Mars: Sorry, You Can't Pack Your Toothbrush Yet," *Science World*, December 8, 2003.

René Ebersole, "North to Mars," *Current Science*, March 1, 2002.

Edmund A. Fortier and Chesley Bonestell, "The Mars That Never Was," *Astronomy*, December 1995.

Scott Lafee, "The Mars Collection," *New Scientist*, September 2, 2000.

Oliver Morton, "Mars: Planet Ice," *National Geographic*, January 2004.

Web Sites

How Mars Works (http://science.howstuffworks.com/mars.htm). Includes a wealth of information about the planet Mars and the missions undertaken to explore it.

National Aeronautics and Space Administration (www. nasa.gov). An outstanding resource that provides facts, figures, illustrations, photographs, articles, mission details, and updates, basically everything astronomy fans want to know about Mars exploration. Visitors can link to the JPL site, the Science@NASA site, and special areas designed just for students.

NOVA (www.pbs.org/wgbh/nova). A search for "Mars" at this site (based on the PBS series) provides visitors with an excellent array of articles about the red planet, as well as animated reenactments of how rovers journey from Earth to Mars.

Space.com (www.space.com). An excellent collection of space-related material, including much information about Mars exploration and missions.

Space Today (www.spacetoday.org). Another information-packed site that provides visitors with a wealth of interesting data about past, present, and future space exploration.

Works Consulted

Books

Isaac Asimov, *Mars: The Red Planet.* New York: Lothrop, Lee & Shepard, 1977. Written by an author long revered for his scientific writings, this is a study of Mars from the earliest discoveries through the *Viking* mission in 1976.

Joseph M. Boyce, *The Smithsonian Book of Mars.* Washington, DC, and London: Smithsonian Institution Press, 2002. A well-researched, detailed book that discusses Mars's climate, atmosphere, surface, and interior, as well as giving in-depth descriptions of space missions. Highly recommended.

Robert Godwin, ed., *Mars: The NASA Mission Reports.* Burlington, ON: Apogee, 2000. An excellent resource that includes actual Mars mission reports, details of spacecraft, and other information released by NASA.

Paul Raeburn, *Uncovering the Secrets of the Red Planet.* Washington, DC: National Geographic Society, 1998. An interesting, enlightening, and easy-to-read book written by an award-winning science journalist. Highly recommended.

Carl Sagan, *Cosmos.* New York: Wings, 1995. A book based on the late scientist's well-known television series of the same name, told in a way that makes space exploration come to life for the reader.

William Sheehan, *The Planet Mars: A History of Observation and Discovery.* Tucson: University of Arizona Press, 1996. Traces the human fascination with Mars starting with ancient peoples who observed it with the naked eye up through exploration in the 1990s.

William Sheehan and Stephen James O'Meara, *Mars: The Lure of the Red Planet.* Amherst, NY: Prometheus, 2001. Provides information and details about everything from ancient astronomers and their fascination with Mars to current space missions.

Robert Zubrin, *The Case for Mars: The Plan to Settle the Red Planet and Why We Must.* New York: Free Press, 1996. A book by a leading space exploration authority who has developed a very detailed "blueprint" for sending humans to Mars.

Periodicals

David S.F. Portree, "The New Martian Chronicles," *Astronomy,* August 1997.

Wernher von Braun, "The Next 20 Years of Interplanetary Exploration," *Astronautics & Aeronautics,* November 1965.

Internet Sources

Jonathan Amos, "Ankle-Deep on Mars," *BBC News,* February 16, 2003. http://news.bbc.co.uk/1/hi/in_depth/sci_tech/2003/denver_2003/2769589.stm. An interesting article about the ice that was discovered by the *Mars Odyssey* rover in 2003.

Charlene Anderson, "The First Rover on Mars: The Soviets Did It in 1971," *Planetary Report,* July/August 1990. www.planetary.org/mars/tpr_rover-rus_first-rover.html. An article about the secretive Mars rover/lander mission of the Soviet Union in 1971.

Bill Arnett, "Mars," NinePlanets.org, March 19, 2004. www.nineplanets.org/mars.html. An informative online article about the red planet that includes links to many different Mars-related sites, including a vast collection of images.

Sallie Baliunas, "Close Encounter," *Tech Central Station,* August 15, 2003. www.techcentralstation.com/081503B.html. Discusses how "Mars Fever" swept through the world during the days of Percival Lowell.

Marshall Brain, "How the Mars Exploration Rovers Work," *How*

Stuff Works. http://science.howstuffworks.com/mars-rover. htm. A wonderful, in-depth article about the *Spirit* and *Opportunity* rovers and their Mars mission.

Robert Roy Britt, "Sand Dunes on Mars Reach Dizzying Heights," *Space.com*, November 10, 2003. www.space.com/ scienceastronomy/mystery_monday_031110.html. A fascinating article about Martian sand dunes.

Adam P. Bruckner, "How Humans Can Get to Mars," 1998. http://more.abcnews.go.com/sections/scitech/marsorbust/ mars_how.html. An article about the challenges of sending humans to the red planet.

George W. Bush, "President Bush Announces New Vision for Space Exploration Program," White House press release, January 14, 2004. www.whitehouse.gov/news/releases/2004/ 01/20040114-3.html.

Ricaurte Chock, "*Pathfinder* Mission and Mars Landing," NASA Glenn Research Center, Photovoltaic and Space Experiments Branch, August 7, 2002. http://powerweb.grc.nasa.gov.

Greg Clark, "Will Nuclear Power Put Humans on Mars?" *Space.com*, May 21, 2000. www.space.com/scienceastronomy/solarsystem/nuclearmars_000521.html. An article about how nuclear technology could be the answer for lower-cost missions to Mars.

David J. Craig, "The Air Up There: BU Planetary Scientist Tracks *Spirit*'s Trip to Mars," *BU Bridge*, January 16, 2004. www. bu.edu/bridge/archive/2004/01-16/mars.html. A planetary scientist involved in the *Mars Exploration Rover* mission describes the Martian atmosphere.

Anthony R. Curtis, "Exploring Mars!" *Space Today*. www.space today.org/SolSys/Mars/Mars.html. A comprehensive and well-written collection of information about Mars the planet and Mars exploration.

Leonard David, "Mars Rovers in Autumn: A Life-and-Death Drama on the Red Planet," *Space.com Space Flight*, May 6,

2004. www.space.com/missionlaunches/rovers_autumn_040 506.html. A look at the *Spirit* and *Opportunity* rovers.

European Space Agency, "Mars vs Earth," *Science & Technology*, July 7, 2003. http://sci.esa.int/science-e/www/object/index. cfm?fobjectid=31025. Interesting information about the contrast between Mars and Earth.

————, "Martian Interior: Volcanism," *Science & Technology*, June 2, 2004. http://sci.esa.int/science-e/www/object/index.cfm? fobjectid=31028&fbodylongid=646. An examination of the geological processes that shaped Mars.

Calvin J. Hamilton, "History of Space Exploration." www.solar views.com/eng/history.htm. An excellent resource that answers virtually any question about Mars from the past to the present.

Stephen J. Hoffman and David L. Kaplan, "Human Exploration of Mars: The Reference Mission of the NASA Mars Exploration Study Team," NASA, July 1997. http://exploration.jsc.nasa. gov/marsref/Mars1txt.pdf. A comprehensive report explaining what it would take to send human explorers to Mars.

Paul Karol and David Catling, *Planet Mars Chronology*, 1996. www-mgcm.arc.nasa.gov/mgcm/fun/mars_chro.html. A good timeline of Mars exploration.

John F. Kennedy, "Special Message to the Congress on Urgent National Needs," May 25, 1961, John F. Kennedy Library and Museum. www.cs.umb.edu/jfklibrary. The complete text of President Kennedy's speech in which he stressed the need for space exploration.

Karen Miller, "Mars Mice," Science@NASA, January 20, 2004. http://science.nasa.gov/headlines/y2004/20jan_marsmice.htm. Discusses NASA's plan to send mice astronauts to Mars in 2006.

Karen Miller and Tony Phillips, "Harvesting Mars," Science @NASA, August 26, 2003. http://science.nasa.gov/headlines/ y2OO3/20aug_supercriticalco2.htm. An intriguing account of how astronauts visiting Mars will have to live off the land.

NASA, "From Robot Geologists to Human Geologists on Mars," *Mars Exploration Rover Mission*, January 13, 2004. http://mars rover.jpl.nasa.gov/spotlight/spirit/a8_20040113.html.

——, "Mars Exploration Rover Mission," March 19, 2004. http://marsrovers.jpl.nasa.gov/mission. Excellent, comprehensive collection of articles about the *MER* mission that describe the launch vehicle, landers, and rovers, as well as a step-by-step explanation of the spacecraft's landing on Mars.

Franklin O'Donnell, *JPL 101*, California Institute of Technology, 2002. www.jpl.nasa.gov. A thorough, interesting history of the Jet Propulsion Laboratory.

Tony Phillips, "Can People Go to Mars?" Science@NASA, February 17, 2004. http://science.nasa.gov/headlines/y2004/17feb_radiation.htm. Takes a close look at the radiation risks on Mars for human explorers.

——, "Planet Gobbling Dust Storms," Science@NASA, July 16, 2001. http://science@nasa.gov/headlines/y2001/ast16jul%5F1.htm.

Planetary Society, "The History of Missions to Mars." www.planetary.org/mars/missions-past.html. A detailed chronology of Mars exploration.

Annie Platoff, *Eyes on the Red Planet: Human Mars Mission Planning, 1952–1970*, NASA Technical Publications, July 2001. http://ston.jsc.nasa.gov/collections/TRS/_techrep/CR-2001-208928.pdf. A well-written and interesting account of the many years of planning for a human voyage to Mars.

Emily Sohn, "Destination Mars," *Science News for Kids*, March 17, 2004. www.sciencenewsforkids.org/articles/20040317/Feature1.asp. An article about human expeditions to Mars, including some details about NASA's plans to send mice to the red planet before it sends people.

Space Telescope Science Institute, "Mars' Chaotic Climate," *HubbleSite NewsCenter*, May 20, 1997. http://hubblesite.org/newscenter/newsdesk/archive/releases/1997/15/astrofile.

Describes the radical changes in the Martian climate and weather patterns.

David P. Stern, *From Stargazers to Starships*, 2001. http://pwg. gsfc.nasa.gov/stargaze. A complete online book written by a scientist with a wealth of knowledge about anything related to space exploration.

Kevin Zahnle, "Decline and Fall of the Martian Empire," *Nature*, July 12, 2001. www.stat.rice.edu./~siefert/Pubfiles/Zahnle Mars.pdf.

Index

Picture Credits

About the Author

Peggy J. Parks holds a bachelor of science degree from Aquinas College in Grand Rapids, Michigan, where she graduated magna cum laude. She is a freelance writer and author who has written more than thirty titles for Thomson/Gale's Lucent Books, Blackbirch Press, and KidHaven Press. Her books cover a wide range of topics, including global warming, the Internet, the Great Depression, conflict in the Middle East, notable scientific achievers, famous world landmarks, natural wonders, and careers. Parks lives in Muskegon, Michigan, a town that she says inspires her writing because of its location on the shores of Lake Michigan.